Secrecy, Privacy and Accountability

Mike Sheaff

Secrecy, Privacy and Accountability

Challenges for Social Research

palgrave
macmillan

Mike Sheaff
School of Law, Criminology & Government
University of Plymouth
Plymouth, UK

ISBN 978-3-030-11685-9 ISBN 978-3-030-11686-6 (eBook)
https://doi.org/10.1007/978-3-030-11686-6

This Palgrave Pivot imprint is published by the registered company Springer Nature Switzerland AG
The registered company address is: Gewerbestrasse 11, 6330 Cham, Switzerland

For Fiona, Tristan, Dan, Sherri & Josh

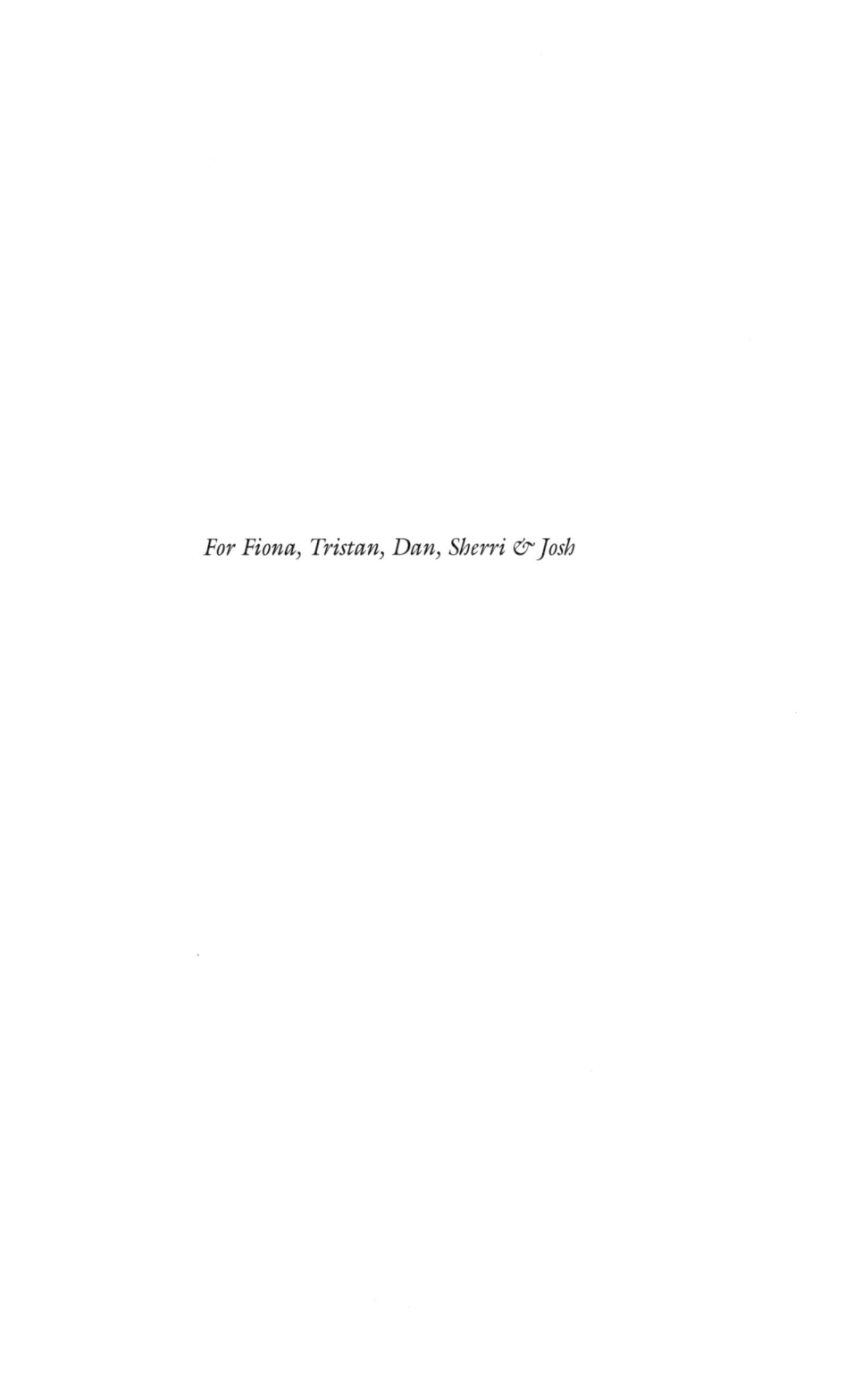

Contents

CHAPTER 1

Introduction

Abstract At a time of declining public trust in power-holders, wider concerns exist over both intrusions into personal privacy and excessive secrecy by those in authority. While privacy is frequently viewed positively, secrecy can generate suspicions of scandal or corruption. One difficulty is that concepts sometimes perceived as a binary divide—secrecy versus transparency or public versus private—possess more permeable and contested boundaries. The introductory chapter sets these issues in a context of organisational failures, using two examples involving child deaths to illustrate media and political approaches to framing responsibility. Referring to UK law on data protection and freedom of information, this introduction sets the scene for later chapters, introducing parallel tensions between privacy and transparency, and between personal responsibility and system failure.

Keywords Trust • Responsibility • Accountability • Blame

'Information is the key to sound decision-making, to accountability and development; it underpins democracy and assists in combatting poverty, oppression, corruption, prejudice and inefficiency' (*Kennedy v The Charity Commission 2014*). Lord Mance's remarks in the UK Supreme Court accompanied the dismissal of an application from a *Times* journalist for

M. Sheaff, *Secrecy, Privacy and Accountability*,
https://doi.org/10.1007/978-3-030-11686-6_1

disclosure of details of a Charity Commission inquiry into the Mariam Appeal, established by a former member of parliament, George Galloway. In his judgment, Lord Mance included a 43-paragraph discussion on how the European Court of Human Rights' case law applied Article 10 of the European Convention on Human Rights (guaranteeing freedom of expression) to rights to access to information. Apparently conflicting decisions were, he observed, 'neither clear nor easy to reconcile'.

These issues form the background to this book, which explores use of freedom of information legislation in social research, with a particular focus on the conflict this can generate with rights to privacy and the protection of personal information. Difficulties in establishing clarity in jurisprudence reflect the intensely socially contested character of underlying issues. An important context is the tension between pervasive concerns about threats to privacy and simultaneous suspicions of concealment and deception by those in authority. As I write this, in late December 2018, there have been widespread media reports of a couple arrested at Gatwick airport just before Christmas on suspicion of flying a drone disrupting travel plans of thousands. Released without charge, their arrest had received prominent media attention, including a *Mail on Sunday* front-page on 23 December displaying a photograph of them alongside the headline, 'ARE THESE THE MORONS WHO RUINED CHRISTMAS?' One of the couple later explained to a newspaper their feeling of being 'violated', adding, 'our home has been searched and our privacy and identity completely exposed … We are deeply distressed, as are our family and friends, and we are receiving medical care' (Kelner 2018).

On 6 December, the *Daily Mail* ran a front-page headline: 'IS <u>NOTHING</u> PRIVATE ANYMORE?' On the same day other headlines included:

'HOW FACEBOOK SPIED ON YOU … AND YOUR PALS.' (*Metro*)
'Facebook discussed cashing in on user data, emails show.' (*The Guardian*)

The *Daily Mail* story ranged wider, but most were prompted by release of confidential emails between senior figures at Facebook by a House of Commons committee investigating 'fake news'. Contested boundaries between media investigation and intrusion have definitions of 'public interest' at their core. This contestation reflects its socially constructed character in a period of mistrust in authority. Such mistrust exists across many dimensions. Two days before these news stories, for the first time in modern British parliamentary history, government Ministers were held to be in contempt of parliament by the House of Commons for failing to publish the full Attorney General's legal advice on the EU Withdrawal Agreement. The sharing and disclosure of information has long been a significant source of conflict, but this intensifies as developments in digital technology make its collection and storage so much easier. One particular feature of this landscape is explored in this book. This concerns the relationship between transparency and accountability on the one side, and secrecy and personal privacy on the other. Specifically, it develops a discussion on opportunities for social research to use Freedom of Information Act (FOIA) requests as a method, and tensions this may generate with the protection of 'personal information' under the Data Protection Act.[1] Through this, the boundary between 'public information' and 'personal information' becomes a contested area.

It is a truism to describe our age as one of declining public trust in authority, fed by suspicion of scandal and corruption. Meanwhile, with dominant neoliberal discourses of responsibility and transparency, our public reputations become commodities, marketable through the type of 'impression management' described in a very different time by Goffman (1959). Successful outcomes are what matter, as 'personal branding' keeps failures 'back-stage'. But this is an unequal process. Becker used the term 'hierarchy of credibility' to describe circumstances where 'members of the highest group have the right to define the way things really are' (Becker 1967: 241). For some, constructions of the 'neoliberal self', 'transforms civil society, in that citizens are constituted as individuals whose identities must be defined in and through the marketplace, whose influence comes to pervade all social domains' (Vallas and Cummins 2015: 297). While there is a considerable research literature suggesting the 'enterprising self' model did not get internalised to the extent some predicted (see Watson 2008), it nonetheless provides one influential form of discourse that can be 'received and interpreted in the particular and complex contexts that individuals move through in their everyday lives' (Halford and Leonard 2006: 658). In these contexts, an uncertain boundary can develop between the safeguarding of privacy and the protection of what Goffman called

[1]The General Data Protection Regulations led to changes in the Data Protection Act in 2018. The law provides an important focus for this book, but it is not a law text, and as the principles underpinning the legislation remain the same, these changes to the DPA are not discussed.

'dark secrets' (Goffman 1959). If privacy mutates into secrecy, generating further public mistrust, the cycle continues. A consequence has been populist attacks on elites accompanied by allegations of 'fake news' from the 'Mainstream Media'. Secrecy by those in authority is matched by suspicion among the public: 'they're all the same', 'they're corrupt' and so on. And when things go wrong, as they will, the immediate response from those in charge all too often appears defensive and self-serving. No doubt prompted by fear of media and public hostility, it merely compounds the problem.

Failures are not scandals. Nor are errors a signal of corruption. While there can be many reasons for conflation of these categories, a route to disentangling them is to consider the close relationship between two issues: implications of the public/private boundary for personal privacy and public accountability; and constructions of explanations for failures in organisation in terms of people and systems. In exploring these themes, this book suggests a contribution by social research to these debates. Although the distinction between 'public' and 'private' has been described as 'a central and characteristic preoccupation of Western thought since antiquity' (Weintraub 1997: 1), it is a complex and not a straightforward binary division. Discussing alternative approaches, Weintraub notes how these 'reflect deeper differences in both theoretical and ideological commitments, in sociological assumptions, and/or in sociohistorical context. Partly for these reasons, debates about how to cut up the social world between public and private are rarely innocent analytical exercises, since they often carry powerful normative implications' (Weintraub 1997: 3).

An underlying theme in this book, the decline of public trust in those holding positions of authority, is examined through a lens that focuses on a paradox in the neoliberal project, between 'responsibilization' and transparency. Support for both principles extends beyond neoliberalism, but more distinctive is the model of the 'enterprising' or 'entrepreneurial self'. Public debate on how much other people should know of our actions and decisions is frequently cast in terms of surveillance, Big Data and the like, an issue I address, but my main interest is rather different. It concerns the transparency of actions performed, not by private citizens, but by public officials and those in authority, bringing questions about the boundary between the public and the private centre-stage.

As context for later discussion on the 'responsible self', I begin with two examples, both involving the deaths of young children:

> There are no words strong enough to express *Sun* readers' anger at the buck passing and blame-dodging over the horrific death of Baby P … Sun readers demand SACKINGS for all who share responsibility for allowing Baby P's appalling death … Heads must roll. Nothing else will do. Sharon Shoesmith, the smug Haringey director of children's services, must be fired. (*The Sun*, 13 November 2008)

> 'How can she live with herself?' – Mother of Down's syndrome boy who died from sepsis slams 'disgusting' decision to let doctor convicted of his manslaughter to work again'. (*Daily Mail*, 14 August 2018)

Deaths of children are among the hardest of events to comprehend or explain. If it appears they could have been avoided, sadness and despair will easily turn to anger. The following account considers ways in which questions of personal errors, culpability and system failure were constructed, starting with Peter Connelly (Baby P) who died aged just seventeen months in August 2007 having suffered over fifty injuries. These were received during a period when he had regular contact with the National Health Service (NHS) and the local authority children's department. Urging action to identify those holding organisational responsibility, David Cameron MP, then Leader of the Opposition, wrote in the London *Evening Standard*, 'We've had a raft of excuses and not one apology. Everyone says they followed protocol to the letter and that the fault lies with some systemic failure. But we cannot allow the words "systemic failure" to absolve anyone of responsibility. Systems are made up of people and the buck has got to stop somewhere' (quoted in Warner 2015: 31–32).

The theme was continued the following day, with a *Daily Mail* editorial lambasting professionals, managers and politicians whose, 'only thought, it appears, is to insist that "correct procedures" were followed … Baby P's case is a damning indictment of a bureaucratic system that could almost have been designed to ensure buck-passing … The guilty must be identified, heads must roll and the mistakes which led to Baby P's entirely preventable death must never happen again. And Baby P? On his little coffin should be a plaque which bears the legend: 'The correct procedures were followed.''

Within a few weeks, the Secretary of State for Children, Schools and Families, Ed Balls MP, ordered the dismissal of the Haringey Director of Children's Services (DCS) (Gammell 2008). This decision was later declared unlawful by the Court of Appeal in 2011, primarily on the grounds that 'the Secretary of State did not afford Ms Shoesmith the opportunity to put her case' (R (*Shoesmith) v OFSTED and Others, 2011, EWCA Civ 642)*. In forming this view, the Appeal Court noted these comments in a report by OFSTED into Haringey children's services, ordered by Mr Balls MP in November 2008:

> Our concern was how the system worked *as a whole*. We were involved in a wide ranging evidence-gathering exercise in order to try to reach an overall assessment of the way in which the different children's services in Haringey were working, and working together. We were looking across the board at the quality of safeguarding practice at all levels of the relevant organisations. We were not seeking to make, or test, allegations against any particular individuals.

In his judgment, Lord Justice Maurice Kay observed:

> The fact that the 2004 Act, in creating the singular post of DCS, identified as a matter of policy one individual with ultimate responsibility and accountability in relation to children's services does not mean that that person is to be denied the protections that have long been accorded to responsible and accountable office-holders ... "Accountability" is not synonymous with "Heads must roll" ... Accountability requires that the accountable person is obliged to explain the state of affairs to which it attaches. The corollary is that there must be a proper opportunity to do so. If the explanation is unacceptable, then consequences will follow. (para 65–66)

An application by the Government seeking leave to appeal this decision was refused by the Supreme Court. Describing his 'surprise and concern' at this decision, Ed Balls expressed a 'fear that the appeal court judgment will now make it very difficult for ministers to act swiftly in the public interest to use their statutory powers when children are at risk, as I did in this case' (Ramesh 2011). Media attention and political pressures can shape constructions of accountabilities in particular ways, and a second example relates to a professional rather than managerial context. Dr Hadiza Bawa-Garba is a paediatrician found guilty of gross negligence manslaughter following the death of a six-year-old patient in February 2011. The Medical Practitioners Tribunal (MPT) suspended her registration from practice for twelve months, after hearing evidence from Dr Bawa-Garba's former supervisor, a consultant neonatologist at Leicester Royal Infirmary:

> who stated that following the events of 18 February 2011, a Trust investigation was carried out which highlighted multiple systemic failures which existed at the time of these events. These included failings on the part of the nurses and consultants, medical and nursing staff shortages, IT system failures which led to abnormal laboratory test results not being highlighted, the deficiencies in handover, accessibility of the data at the bedside, and the absence of a mechanism for an automatic consultant review. The Tribunal therefore determined that whilst your actions fell far short of the standards expected and were a causative factor in the early death of Patient A, they took place in the context of wider failings. (*Hadiza Bawa-Garba and The General Medical Council & others: para 28*)

The General Medical Council (GMC), a body established by statute in 1858, having responsibility to 'protect, promote and maintain the health and safety of the public', appealed this decision. The suspension was overruled by the High Court, which substituted a direction that Dr Bawa-Garba's name be erased from the Medical Register. This was subsequently overturned by the Appeal Court judges, noting how the High Court judge had reasoned, 'although systemic failings or the failings of others may reduce Dr Bawa-Garba's culpability, they could not reduce her failures, which were her personal responsibility' (para 49). In contrast, the Appeal Court judgment held that the MPT was engaged in very different purpose to that of the jury in a criminal trial:

> there was a fundamental difference between the task and necessary approach of the jury, on the one hand, and that of the Tribunal, on the other. The task of the jury was to decide on the guilt or absence of guilt of Dr Bawa-Garba having regard to her past conduct. The task of the Tribunal, looking to the future, was to decide what sanction would most appropriately meet the statutory objective of protecting the public. (*Hadiza Bawa-Garba and The General Medical Council & others: para 76*)

Of many significant issues raised by these examples, two form an important focus in this book. One concerns responsibility, and its division between 'persons' and 'systems', with the other relating to the construction of reputation. Mid-way through the ten years separating these two episodes, the report of a public inquiry into Mid Staffordshire NHS Trust addressed the first of these. The background was a 2007 report indicating an apparently higher mortality rate at Mid Staffs hospital than would be expected, prompting an investigation by the Health Care Commission

(HCC). After a highly critical report published in March 2009, the coalition government established a public inquiry to investigate failures at the hospital. The final report, published in 2013, concluded that even where individual actions may fall short of what should be expected, this needed to be considered in context:

> The evidence to this inquiry has shown that we have still not managed to move successfully away from the culture of blame which Professor Liam Donaldson, in *An Organisation with a Memory*, and Professor Sir Ian Kennedy, in the report of the Bristol inquiry, were so keen to banish. The understandable human need to identify one or more people to be held to account means that whenever something goes wrong a hunt starts, and the larger the disaster the more pressure there is.
>
> There is a tendency when a disaster strikes to try to seek out someone who can be blamed for what occurred, and a public expectation that those held responsible will be held to account … In a system failure as widespread as that identified in this Inquiry, it becomes a futile exercise to undertake; so many are in one sense accountable, it is far more effective to learn rather than to punish. To place too much emphasis on individual blame is to risk perpetuating the illusion that removal of particular individuals is all that is necessary. (Francis 2013: Vol 1, para 106–108)

An Organisation with a Memory, published in 2000, offered a review and recommendations on dealing with organisational failures, describing:

> two ways of viewing human error: the person-centred approach and the system approach. The former is still the most dominant tradition within the academic literature on failure, largely because it is more suited to the agenda of management. This approach focuses on the psychological precursors of error, such as inattention, forgetfulness and carelessness … Aside from treating errors as moral issues, it isolates unsafe acts from their context, thus making it very hard to uncover and eliminate recurrent error traps within the system … It is important to emphasise that this does not mean that individuals should never be held accountable for their actions ….
>
> The system approach, in contrast, takes a holistic stance on the issues of failure. It recognises that many of the problems facing organisations are complex, ill-defined and result from the interaction of a number of factors … Errors are seen as being shaped and provoked by 'upstream' systemic factors, which include the organisation's strategy, its culture and the approach of management towards risk and uncertainty. (Department of Health 2000: 20–21)

This approach was reflected in the analysis offered thirteen years later in the Mid Staffs public inquiry. The episode resulted in the disciplining of some clinical staff by professional bodies, including the hospital's chief nurse who agreed to be struck off the nursing and midwifery register, but there was considerable public disquiet that no non-clinical managers faced disciplinary action. This was a consequence of differing regulatory arrangements for members of health professions, but the inquiry report's reluctance to recommend disciplinary sanctions reflected its conclusion that emphasised the importance of culture: 'Much will be said about culture in the report. Individuals and indeed organisations acting in accordance with a culture, even a negative or unhealthy one, cannot always be held personally responsible for doing so' (Francis 2013: Introduction, para 112, pp. 36–7). This brings the connection between what is public and what is personal, and constructions of boundaries between them, right back to the centre, a theme developed further in Chap. 2.

Another important contextual factor is the statutory basis on which information about individuals and public authorities is held. One involves the DPA, which brought the European Union's 1995 Data Protection Directive into UK law, providing individuals with legal rights relating to information held about them by organisations. For information about individuals to be processed lawfully, organisations must comply with specified data protection principles. The other is the FOIA which came into effect in 2005. It applies to central and local government, NHS organisations and other bodies from Universities to the Charity Commission. Writing in the Preface to the 1997 White Paper preceding the Bill, the Prime Minister, Tony Blair, foresaw, 'a fundamental and vital change in the relationship between government and governed'. He continued: 'The traditional culture of secrecy will only be broken down by giving people in the United Kingdom a legal right to know. This fundamental and vital change in the relationship between government and governed is at the heart of the White Paper' (Chancellor of the Duchy of Lancaster 1998). The Information Commissioner estimated that by the middle of 2009, approximately 500,000 requests had been made. The law provides for exemptions allowing public authorities to refuse disclosure, seventeen of which are qualified, meaning they are subject to a public interest test. This requires a balance to be made between the organisation's reasons for non-disclosure and a public interest in disclosure. Seven are absolute exemptions, intended to apply without qualification. Where an organisation refuses to disclose, the applicant may request an internal review, and if remaining dissatisfied can take a complaint to the ICO who following investigation issues a Decision Notice (DN). From there, an appeal, by either party, can be made to the Information Tribunal.

One of the absolute exemptions, for 'personal' information, under s40 of the Act, includes two kinds. s40(1) concerns 'personal data of which the applicant is the data subject'. In other words, you cannot seek disclosure of information held by a public authority about yourself through a FOIA request. For this, the appropriate route is a subject access request under the Data Protection Act 1998 (DPA). s40(2) is less straightforward, relating to protection of personal data of a third party under the DPA. There has been an increasing use of s40 as a justification for non-disclosure by central government departments: increasing from 24.9% of refusals in 2005 (Department for Constitutional Affairs 2006), to 47.1% in 2017 (Cabinet Office 2018). This increase provided one stimulus for considering the value of FOIA as a research tool in the context of the exemption of 'personal' information. FOIA is about transparency, while DPA is about privacy, concepts providing the focus for the next two chapters.

There is one further way in which the public and the personal are connected in this book. This concerns my own involvement in a public role that was the source of research I describe in Chap. 5. One issue it required me to address was whether this brought me too close to the object of my study. Writings of Carolyn Ellis stimulated me to consider the contribution 'sociological introspection' (Ellis 1991) might make, and more broadly, Gayle Letherby, Julie Parsons and others encouraged me to develop my thinking about how this connects with ideas about objectivity and subjectivity. Letherby (2013) refers to this comment by C Wright Mills: 'learn to use your life experience in your intellectual work; continually to examine and interpret it' (Mills 1959: 216). Elsewhere, Anderson draws a contrast between 'evocative auto-ethnography', which can successfully convey the feelings and emotions of an experience, and 'analytic auto-ethnography', in which autobiographical experiences are used as a resource for more systematic investigation (Anderson 2006). This was what I hoped to do, but I realised I had to first acknowledge a point made by Letherby, to start, 'by accepting our subjective position – the significance of our personhood (intellectual and personal) within the research process – and really try to understand the complexities and the influence of these' (Letherby 2013: 87). I return to this in the final section of Chap. 5.

Interests in organisational failure and the exercise of power stimulated my interest in exploring use of FOIA as a research method in social research, prompted also by Laura Nader's call for 'studying-up', urging that research should not only 'study-down' … 'a reinvented anthropology should study powerful institutions and bureaucratic organisations' (Nader 1969/1972: 292). I hope ideas shared in this book will stimulate thinking and discussion in an area that would benefit from greater attention.

References

Anderson, L. (2006). Analytic Autoethnography. *Journal of Contemporary Ethnography, 35*, 373–395.

Becker, H. (1967). Whose Side Are We On? *Social Problems, 14*(3), 234–247.

Cabinet Office. (2018). *Freedom of Information Statistics in Central Government for 2017*. London: Cabinet Office.

Chancellor of the Duchy of Lancaster. (1998). *Your Right to Know. White Paper*. London: The Stationery Office.

Department for Constitutional Affairs. (2006). *Freedom of Information Annual Report 2005: Operation of the FOI Act in Central Government*. London: Department for Constitutional Affairs.

Department of Health. (2000). *An Organisation with a Memory*. London: Department of Health.

Ellis, C. (1991). Sociological Introspection and Emotional Experience. *Symbolic Interaction, 14*(1), 23–50.

Francis, R. (2013). *Report of the Mid Staffordshire NHS Foundation Trust Public Inquiry*. London: The Stationery Office.

Gammell, C. (2008, December 8). Sharon Shoesmith Sacked After Baby P Scandal. *The Daily Telegraph*.

Goffman, E. (1959/1990). *The Presentation of Self in Everyday Life*. London: Penguin.

Halford, S., & Leonard, P. (2006). Place, Space and Time: Contextualizing Workplace Subjectivities. *Organization Studies, 27*(5), 657–676.

Kelner, S. (2018, December 26). The Case of Paul Gait and Elaine Kirt Shows That the Rush to Judgement Can Make Morons of Us All. *iNews*.

Letherby, G. (2013). Theorised Subjectivity. In G. Letherby, J. Scott, & M. Williams (Eds.), *Objectivity and Subjectivity in Social Research*. London: Sage.

Mills, C. W. (1959/2000). *The Sociological Imagination*. Oxford: Oxford University Press.

Nader, L. (1969/1972). Up the Anthropologist: Perspectives Gained from Studying Up. In D. Hymes (Ed.), *Reinventing Anthropology*. New York: Random House.

Ramesh, R. (2011, August 2). Supreme Court Rejects Bid to Challenge Ruling on Sharon Shoesmith Sacking. *The Guardian.*

Vallas, S. P., & Cummins, E. R. (2015). Personal Branding and Identity Norms in the Popular Business Press: Enterprise Culture in an Age of Precarity. *Organization Studies, 36*(3), 293–319.

Warner, J. (2015). *The Emotional Politics of Social Work and Child Protection.* Bristol: Policy Press.

Watson, T. J. (2008). Managing Identity: Identity Work, Personal Predicaments and Structural Circumstances. *Organization, 15*(1), 121–143.

Weintraub, J. (1997). The Theory and Politics of the Public/Private Distinction. In Weintraub and Kumar (Eds.).

CHAPTER 2

Public and Private: Transparency and Responsibility

Abstract The long-contested boundary between 'public' and 'private' spheres gains renewed relevance as ideas of transparency and responsibility come to the fore in public policy discourse. These issues have special importance for understanding organisational failure, sometimes presented in terms of another binary, between 'people' and 'systems'. With public mistrust of those in authority increasing, this chapter considers examples of past sociological studies of disasters to illustrate differing ways in which questions of responsibility and blame are addressed. Detailed attention is given to this in the context of the 1966 Aberfan disaster. The chapter ends by suggesting that while contemporary neoliberal discourses apparently favour responsibility and transparency, tensions between them, accompanied by uncertain boundaries between privacy and secrecy, can create a retreat from both.

Keywords Transparency • Responsibility • Neoliberal • Entrepreneurial • Public-private

Sociology, notes Brewer, 'has been replete with articles discussing the public-private distinction', with the division moving from an antimony to a 'blurred binary' (Brewer 2005: 661). The contribution of feminist writers has been of special importance. Holmes (2000) describes the impact of second-wave feminism in encouraging attention to 'the personal' (e.g. Seidman 1994),

M. Sheaff, *Secrecy, Privacy and Accountability*,
https://doi.org/10.1007/978-3-030-11686-6_2

expressed in the slogan, 'the personal is political'. Feminism brought this personal domain into the 'sphere of justice and public decision-making', acknowledging that, 'public and private are not real and absolute territories' (Holmes 2000: 307). Constructing the definition of private as equivalent to domestic, this however tended to ignore other features of 'private' within civil society (Pateman 1989). 'Feminist definitions of public and private may have had their limitations but feminists were clear and critical in their recognition that it was the constructed dichotomy between the two that needed challenging' (Holmes 2000: 307).

Bailey describes the connection between the public and the private as 'an insistent sub-text in the history of sociological thought, though it has rarely been explicated or phrased in precisely those terms' (Bailey 2000: 386). Reviewing shifts in focus within the discipline, he notes how concerns about a decline in the vitality of public life, and perceptions of public disillusion and disengagement from the public word, have been accompanied by strengthening interests in identity, the self, emotions and intimacy. Bailey also explores influences shaping these interests, notably the Frankfurt School, Freud and psychoanalysis, Foucault, Feminism and 'the everyday' (as in the work of Goffman, and ethnomethodology). What we feel and think is grounded in our social experiences, 'but the act of experience, of sentience and of feeling is individual and, in a basic sense, private' (Bailey 2000: 390). Bailey proposed 'three dimensions of the sociological private'—intimate relationships, the unconscious and the self—an approach that met criticism, in particular for subsuming 'family, domestic and friendship relationships' under a framework established around 'the interior life of individuals and intimate relationships' (Ribbens-McCarthy and Edwards 2001: 773). Ribbens-McCarthy and Edwards argue for an understanding of 'the personal' as a way of 'rescuing the private from a total identification with intimacy and the self. Within this approach, we use both the public and the private to refer to social lives and social settings, since they are both concerned with interactions and interdependencies between people in variable locations, and the sets and meanings and experiences that are associated with these' (Ribbens-McCarthy and Edwards 2001: 773).

This also offers a valuable insight for thinking about circumstances where things go wrong in organisations. In an early discussion on organisational failure, focusing upon the handling of intelligence (as information), Wilensky observed how shared attitudes and understandings between social actors in organisations, including regulatory bodies, can contribute to a 'failure of foresight' (Wilensky 1967: 121). And as Durkheim suggested, it is mistaken to regard such shared beliefs and assumptions as purely private: 'The totality of beliefs and sentiments common to the average members of a society forms a determinate system with a life of its own. It can be termed the collective or common consciousness.... it is something totally different from the consciousness of individuals, although it is only realised in individuals' (Durkheim 1893/1997: 38–39).

Developing this idea, Zerubavel rejects 'cognitive individualism', urging instead adoption of a 'cognitive sociology' which 'keeps reminding us that while we certainly think both as individuals and as human beings, what goes on inside our heads is also affected by the particular *thought communities* to which we happen to belong' (Zerubavel 1997: 8–9, emphasis in original). Relatedly, Morgan (1986) uses the metaphor of 'psychic prison' to describe circumstances where: 'organizations and their members can become enmeshed in cognitive traps. False assumptions, taken-for-granted beliefs, unquestioned operating rules, and numerous other premises and practices can combine to create self-contained views of the world' (Morgan 1986: 202). Morgan adds, 'the metaphor shows us that we have over-rationalized our understanding of organization' (Morgan 1986: 228–229).

The active relationship between social setting and individual consciousness is considered in Wacquant's (1992) discussion on 'the dialectic of social and mental structures', in which he refers to Bordieu's concept of habitus as 'a structuring mechanism that operates from within agents, though it is neither strictly individual nor in itself fully determinative of conduct' (Wacquant 1992: 18). As Bourdieu put it, 'the familiar world tends to be "taken for granted," perceived as natural ... the dispositions of agents, their habitus, that is, the mental structures through which they apprehend the social world, are essentially the product of the internalization of the structures of that world' (Bourdieu 1989: 18). All of this work, highlighting difficulties in using a public/private dichotomy, is a reminder that the construction of our sense of self and identity is a social process. Notwithstanding criticisms, Bailey's three dimensions offer a useful framework for discussion here. On intimacy, Bailey argues that while there are emotional dimensions in many relationships, those 'with family members, partners and chosen friends involve the baring of emotional needs and nature to others; trusting and risking at various levels of intensity' (Bailey 2000: 391). This aspect attracted particular attention from Ribbens-McCarthy and Edwards, but it is Bailey's reference to the self that has most relevance for issues considered in this book. Describing the 'conscious, reflective and reflexive self', Bailey identifies modern preoccupations with self-identity and social position: 'Self-interestedness, self-reliance, self-realisation, self-determination and selfishness are all dimensions of a developing and particular privatism which now has associated organisational and institutional forms in the widely-available practices of "personal growth", therapy and counselling' (Bailey 2000: 392). These specific examples are not a focus for this discussion, but they connect with issues of self-identity in the neoliberal era, notions of the 'enterprising self' and the importance of reputation. This introduces further questions about transparency and disclosure of 'personal' information in the context of a disputed private/public boundary.

Private and Public: Visibility and Transparency

In *Keywords*, Raymond Williams notes the origin of the word 'person' in the thirteenth century from persona, observing 'Persona had already gone through a remarkable development, from its earliest meaning of a mask used by a player, through a character in a play and a part that a man acts, to a general word for human being'. Williams also charts the changing meaning of the word 'private', referring in the fourteenth century to a state of being, 'withdrawn from public life', and coming to acquire, 'the sense of secret and concealed both in politics and in the sexual sense of private parts', before leading to what 'we would now recognize as individual and private' (Williams 1983: 233). By the eighteenth and nineteenth centuries, the term '*the* individual', as 'a fundamental order of being', replaced '*an* individual', describing a 'single example of a group' (Williams 1983: 163). This brought accompanying changes: 'a personality or a character, once an outward sign, has been decisively internalized, yet *internalized as a possession, and therefore as something which can be either displayed or interpreted*' (Williams 1983: 178, emphasis added). Referring to Simmel's distinction between *Einzelheit*, as 'singleness' or 'abstract individualism' (one among many of the same kind), and *Einzigheit*, 'the individualism of uniqueness' (only one of a kind), Williams suggests many arguments about 'the individual', 'confuse the distinct senses to which individualism and individuality point', with individualism as a '19th century coinage', a 'theory not only of abstract individuals but of the primacy of individual states and interests' (Williams 1983: 165).

Thompson (2011) develops a related theme, addressing the importance of visibility for defining the public realm in ancient Greece, and using work of Arendt and Habermas to argue that in contemporary society modern communications systems create *mediated visibility*: 'One no longer has to be present in the same spatial-temporal setting in order to see the other individual or to witness the action or event' (Thompson 2011: 56). This is accompanied by a transformation of privacy. Thompson suggests our ideas on what this involves are shaped by liberal-democratic ideas on the importance of the individual and the limits of the state, rather than Ancient Greek notions of the private, concerning 'privation' from the public realm. 'There is', wrote John Stuart Mill in his 1848 *Principles of Political Economy*, 'a circle around every individual human being, which no government ... ought to be permitted to overstep: there is a part of the life of every person ... within which the individuality of that person ought to reign uncontrolled either by any other individual or by the public collectively ... the point to be determined is, where the limit should be placed; how large a province of human life this reserved territory should include' (Mill and Lerner, 1965: 938).

These uncertainties and conflicts remain. Drawing upon Rossler (2005) and Goffman (1972), Thompson describes the private as consisting of 'those territories of the self, which include the environment of the self and information about the self, over which the individual seeks to exercise control and to restrict access by others' (Thompson 2011: 61). However, he goes on to argue:

> the fact that individuals believe that they can and should be able to exercise control over information about themselves does not necessarily mean that they always have the right to do so, or that any right to privacy they have will always trump other considerations. On the contrary, the right to privacy is but one right, and in particular cases it may well be over-ridden by other factors that weigh more heavily in a normative deliberation on the relative merits of conflicting rights and claims. (Thompson 2011: 63)

Thompson argues that while the public-private distinction has been with us for two millennia, changes in the way these concepts are understood cause the boundaries between them to become 'sites of struggle'. 'The shifting boundaries between public and private life become a new battleground in modern societies, a contested terrain where individuals and organizations wage a new kind of information war' (Thompson 2011: 64). This point can be developed through insights offered by scholarship on governance inspired by the work of Foucault. Much of this has addressed processes focused on the construction of our sense of self. For example: 'The key feature of the neo-liberal rationality is the congruence it endeavours to achieve between a responsible and moral individual and an economic-rational actor. It aspires to construct prudent subjects whose moral quality is based on the fact that they rationally assess the costs and benefits of a certain act as opposed to other alternative acts' (Lemke 2001: 201). The desired 'transformation of citizens into self-steering, economically independent, responsibility taking agents' (Pyysiainen et al. 2017: 216) sought to 'link a reduction in (welfare) state services and security systems to the increasing call for "personal responsibility" and "self-care"' (Lemke 2001: 2013).

Alongside notions of enhanced personal responsibility are ones of autonomy. McNay notes how Foucault's remarks about 'the remodelling of the subjective experience of the self around an economized notion of enterprise' bring individual autonomy to the centre of disciplinary control (McNay 2009: 62). One form of this responsible and autonomous self has been the model of the 'enterprising self' (Rose 1992; Peters 2001; McNay 2009). However, this presents significant challenges, as McGuigan (2014) describes with reference to the argument of Ulrich Beck and Elisabeth Beck-Gurnsheim (2001/2002) that individuals are compelled to make agonistic choices through their life-course, having to take sole responsibility for the consequences. 'Individualisation is a matter of institutionalised obligations, not free choice ... The individual is penalised harshly not only for personal failure but for sheer bad luck in a highly competitive and relentlessly harsh social environment' (McGuigan 2014: 233–234). Similarly:

> These neoliberal discourses can be understood as providing 'frames' (or reframings), which incorporate a *diagnosis* or *representation* of a problem situation – including an attribution of blame or causality, and a *prognosis or intervention* that suggests a solution ... neoliberal discourses set out to reframe and re-configure the conditions so that the fate of the agents – and the consequences of their undertakings – would depend predominantly on their own decisions, actions and abilities. Then, as put by Lemke, 'the consequences of the action are borne by the subject alone, who is also solely responsible for them.' (Pyysiainen et al. 2017: 218)

These threats are considered by Davies (2015), whose view is that market uncertainties ultimately require control that is constructed in ways that reflect 'varying assumptions regarding the individual's capacity to cope with a state of constant, uninterrupted flow' (Davies 2015: 40). Davies draws upon a 1992 essay by Deleuze who suggested that disciplinary societies, providing the source for much of Foucault's analysis, were giving way to 'societies of control', in which 'the operation of markets is now the instrument of social control' as 'marketing has become the centre or "soul" of the corporation' (Deleuze 1992: 6). Davies develops this, but comments that the emerging discourse considers 'most individuals require steering in some way, while a small minority of leaders and entrepreneurs can perform the navigation' (Davies 2015: 40). He continues, 'in the light of Deleuze's essay, perhaps we can re-frame neoliberalism as a project which seeks to accelerate the shift from discipline to control, in which markets are simply the best available technologies for this, with entrepreneurship the idealised mode of subjectivity for the control society' (Davies 2015: 43).

The virtues of entrepreneurship and the model of the 'entrepreneurial self' gained increasing expression in British political discourse towards the later part of the twentieth century. In 1999, speaking to the British Venture Capitalists Association, the Prime Minister, Tony Blair, complained of 'the scars on my back' resulting from two years trying to reform the public sector. Blair asserted, 'People in the public sector are more rooted in the concept that "if it's always done this way, it must always be done this way" than any group of people I've come across' (Quoted in Assinder 1999). Soon an alternative style was advocated, with a government White Paper in 2006 foreseeing innovative leaders as key to 'unleashing public sector entrepreneurship' (Secretary of State for Health 2006: 173).

'Transparency is a very popular concept', remarked Etzioni (2010: 15). It is another concept associated with neoliberal discourse, although one that receives support from many whose rationale is drawn from very different perspectives. For Foucault, an important theme of the Enlightenment was its challenge to official secrecy: 'It sought to break up the patches of darkness that blocked the light, eliminate the shadowy areas of society, demolish the unlit chambers where arbitrary political acts, monarchical caprice, religious superstitions, tyrannical and priestly plots, epidemics and the illusions of ignorance were fomented' (Foucault 1980: 153). Meijer notes that Rousseau 'equated opaqueness with evil and considered transparency as the way back to the lost state of nature', adding that 'the idea that people behave correctly when they are being watched can be traced back to Bentham's "panopticon"' (Meijer 2014: 509). In this way, transparency and responsibility are connected: 'it reflects the idea that people are autonomous rational choosers who can govern themselves' (Etzioni 2010: 15).

Etzioni draws a distinction between transparency in the economic realm, whereby consumer sovereignty is exercised through informed choice, and in the public realm, where it serves to deter corruption and poor performance, also quoting Jeremy Bentham, 'the more strictly we are watched, the better we behave' (Etzioni 2010: 4–5). This idea is reflected in the definition of transparency used by Meijer's research team, at the University of Utrecht, as 'the availability of information about an actor allowing other actors to monitor the workings or performance of this actor' (Meijer 2014: 511). This may be achieved pro-actively (through publication of documents), passively (through FOI requests) or through forced access (whistleblowing and leaking). 'All of these forms', it is suggested, 'are argued to contribute to public accountability' (Meijer 2014: 511).

However, within neoliberal discourse, transparency takes particular forms, introduced for specific purposes. For example, in 1997, the Managing Director of the International Monetary Fund (IMF), Michel Camdessus (1997), suggested 'greater transparency will help strengthen market discipline and avoid market surprises that can lead to disruptive market reactions'. Portrayals of an 'audit society' (e.g. Power 1999) and use of 'New Public Management' (NPM), with an emphasis upon targets and performance management, sought to replicate market-driven controls of the corporate boardroom within the public sector. Consequently, it has been suggested 'NPM reforms can be tracked to the ascendancy of neoliberal ideas of the early 1980s' (Simonet 2011: 815). Continuing through New Labour, these objectives were taken further by the Coalition Government between 2010 and 2015. Its approach was explained in a statement on transparency and accountability, reflecting the economic liberalism of Hayek as much as the political liberalism of Rousseau:

> The Government believes that we need to throw open the doors of public bodies, to enable the public to hold politicians and public bodies to account. We also recognise that this will help to deliver better value for money in public spending, and help us achieve our aim of cutting the record deficit. Setting government data free will bring significant economic benefits by enabling businesses and non-profit organisations to build innovative applications and websites. (HM Government 2010)

In a recent review, Sarah Moore describes the current aim of transparency as being 'to push out online as much state-produced data as possible; the emphasis, in other words, is on the near-instantaneous publication of large volumes of data' (Moore 2018: 417–8). However, Moore suggests that while this allows us to 'find out how many people died at a given hospital, how many London-bound trains turned up on time in January, how many schoolchildren under-performed in a particular exam in 2015 and how much was spent by an MP on taxis … there are some things that are very evidently not on show, namely the structures and principles that underpin official decisions – or, put differently, the state as a system' (Moore 2018: 428). Moore argues that 'the transparency agenda is based on a simplistic conception of the relationship between visibility and public trust that sees the former as a straightforward condition for the latter … future research might examine the tendency within transparency programmes to conceive of the public through the lens of trust, in terms of a problem to be solved rather than a co-participant in the creation of an open society' (Moore 2018: 427). While transparency achieved elevation as an important governance principle, as with the public-private boundary, it too becomes a site of struggle. This has particular implications for the role seen to be played by personal responsibility constructed within neoliberal discourse. The issues themselves are not new, but there have been very significant changes in how these are framed, illustrated in the following examples of disasters that have been the subject of sociological and other inquiry.

Disasters, Responsibility and Blame

In her analysis of the 1986 *Challenger* spaceship disaster, Diane Vaughan points out, 'all causal explanations have implications for control', describing how a focus upon the role of middle managers 'removed from public scrutiny the contributions to the disaster made by top NASA officials, Congress and the White House' (Vaughan 1996: 392). 'Invariably, the politics of blame directs our attention to certain individuals and not others when organizations have failures. Invariably, the accepted explanation is some form of "operator error", isolating in the media spotlight someone responsible for the hands-on work: the captain of the ship, a political functionary, a technician, or middle-level managers' (Vaughan 1996: 392–3).

In his book, *Normal Accidents*, the US sociologist Charles Perrow describes settings where organisational systems are characterised by 'interactive complexity' (such as having several component sections or divisions) and 'tightly coupled', in which 'processes happen very fast, and can't be turned off' (Perrow 1999: 4). Using the example of the 1979 accident at Three Mile Island Nuclear Generating Station, Perrow suggests this combination of factors means some accidents become inevitable. These are what he describes as 'normal accidents'. Complex technologies may create new hazards, but 'technology is not the only culprit however. The organizations that run these risky enterprises often contribute to their own technological failures' (Vaughan 1990: 225). Vaughan refers to the work of British sociologist Barry Turner, whose investigation of accidents and disasters was 'seeking out any systematic organizational patterns that might have preceded these events' (Vaughan 1990: 225). Turner drew upon Wilensky's work on the role that information plays in organisations. For Wilensky, failures in information could be more important than failures in control, noting 'it is remarkable the sociology of complex organisations has so little to say about the conditions that foster the failure of foresight' (Wilensky 1967: 121). Turner (1976) explores lost opportunities for foresight in a review of three British public inquiries into disasters, all involving loss of life: the Aberfan colliery tip collapse (144 deaths in 1966), the collision between an express train and road transporter at Hixon (eleven deaths in 1968), and the fire at Summerland leisure complex on the Isle of Man (fifty deaths in 1974).

As Vaughan summarises Turner's analysis, 'disasters had long incubation periods characterised by a number of discrepant events signalling danger. These events were overlooked or misinterpreted, accumulating unnoticed' (Vaughan 1990: 225). In his study, Turner cites the work of Carr, who in a very early sociological contribution to the analysis of disasters published in 1932 refers to the consequence of a disaster representing 'a catastrophic change … in the functional adequacy of certain cultural artefacts'. Turner notes, 'A failure of foresight may therefore be regarded as the collapse of precautions that had hitherto been regarded culturally as adequate. Small-scale everyday accidents do not provoke a cultural re-evaluation of precautions' (Turner 1976: 380). But the significance attributed to 'small-scale everyday accidents' is itself socially constructed. Scale is not an independently and objectively verifiable gradient. Two of Turner's observations hint at this, both relating to issues of power:

> In two of the cases, individuals outside the principal organizations concerned had foreseen the danger that led to the disaster, and had complained, only to meet with a high-handed or dismissive response. They were fobbed

> off with ambiguous or misleading statements, or subjected to public relations exercises, because it was automatically assumed that the organisations knew better than outsiders about the hazards of the situations with which they were dealing. (Turner 1976: 388)

> Ambiguity and disagreement among several parties about the status and significance of the evidence pointing to possible danger also served to lead to an undervaluing of such evidence, particularly when the more complacent group was also the more powerful one. (Turner 1976: 391)

The 165-page report of the inquiry into the Aberfan disaster (Davies 1967) identifies many examples of early warnings and concerns of this type. It also makes reference to an episode shortly after the disaster, when Lord Robens, Chairman of the National Coal Board (NCB), claimed in a television interview that no-one knew there was a spring underneath the tip (the build-up of water was a significant causal factor in its collapse). His assertion was challenged by local people, and the report comments: 'as Lord Robens himself knew nothing beyond what he was told by others in the calamitous circumstances then prevailing, it was unwise of him to imply at Aberfan that he had knowledge, and it is understandable that his statement was bitterly resented by the residents, who possessed the intimate local knowledge which he lacked' (Davies 1967: 92).

The Aberfan inquiry report also reports comments by counsel for the National Union of Mineworkers, identifying a failure to connect what was known about potential risks with what was being observed at the Aberfan tip:

> The real fault here, in my submission, was *not* anything unforeseeable, nor anything which could not have been prevented by ordinary, economic, sensible precautions ... The trouble basically arose from the lack of communication between those who possessed the knowledge of the existing facts and those who possessed the knowledge of the potential facts. The experts in the Coal Board knew of the potential facts and the potential danger. If they had got someone at the other side of the bridge who could have served them with the day-to-day facts, to which they could have applied their knowledge, then of course there would have been no disaster. (Davies 1967: 81)

Counsel for the Tribunal described the primary cause of the disaster as a lack of policy that might have enabled these pieces of information to be connected, explaining 'personal responsibility is subordinate to confessed failure to have a policy governing pit stability' (Davies 1967: 83). In describing this as subordinate, individuals are not acquitted of responsibility. The report continues, 'having said that the absence of any policy or system regarding tips must operate strongly in favour of all National Coal Board employees whose conduct falls to be considered by us, it does not logically or necessarily follow that all must therefore be absolved from personal responsibility' (Davies 1967: 83). Part IV of the inquiry report has the heading, 'Should anyone be blamed for the Aberfan disaster?' This question provides the focus for seventy-one pages, almost half of the report. In great detail, the report assesses the role of the National Coal Board (NCB), named individual officials of the NCB – right down to the individuals who unloaded the waste onto the tip—the local Borough Council, and the National Union of Mineworkers (NUM). The report concluded, 'blame for the disaster rests upon the National Coal Board. This blame is shared (though in varying degrees) among the National Coal Board headquarters, the South Western Divisional Board, and certain individuals' (Davies 1967: 131). Referring to information available to the NCB on tip stability, the report asks:

> Does it really lie in the mouths of members of the National Coal Board to say that they were wholly ignorant of such a possibility, and are therefore to be excused from having paid no attention to pit stability? And is Mr Sheppard, in particular, entitled so to shield himself from all responsibility? Such questions (which are wholly different from the question of whether they should have foreseen a slip of the magnitude which occurred at Aberfan) calls for only one answer: They cannot be so excused. If, as reasonable men, they had given thought to the matter, they could not fail to have known and realised that, unless proper steps are taken, spoil tips can and do collapse and that, if they do, they may imperil not only the safety of men working upon them but also the persons and property of others. (Davies 1967: 84–85)

The inquiry saw access to information as central in judging responsibility and blame: those who lacked such access did not share the same degree of culpability. For example, the National Union of Mineworkers had been criticised by counsel for the Parents' and Residents' Association for failing to raise concerns. This, it was suggested, was due to the union's fears that if substantial investment was required to relocate the tip, reduced financial viability of the pit might put it at risk of closure. Rejecting this view, the report focuses on the role of knowledge and information: 'Lacking easy access to such expert knowledge, completely reassured by men whom they were entitled to look to and rely upon, and doubtless influenced (though unconsciously) by the thought that their livelihood was involved, in our judgment it would be unrealistic and unfair to blame the Union for doing no more than they did' (Davies 1967: 112).

The Aberfan inquiry report acknowledged that responsibilities within the NCB were 'diffuse', but explained:

> After critical examination of the acts and omissions of a number of people, we have found many degrees of blameworthiness, from very slight to grave. We later single out only those whose conduct was such that our duty constrains us to do so. But, having learnt that the tipping gang and its chargehand (Mr Leslie Davies) have all been bitterly reviled in Aberfan and treated as pariahs, we must make it clear that we absolve them from all blame in the disaster. (Davies 1967: 93)

The report proceeds to consider in detail the role of nine named officials of the NCB, including managers, engineers and others. Judgments include comments such as:

> On the Unit Mechanical Engineer—'In our judgment, therefore, despite his excellent work record and industry and his lack of instruction and knowledge in matters of tip stability, Mr Vivian Thomas cannot be wholly absolved from a measure of blame for the disaster of 1966.' (Davies 1967: 94)

> On the former Group Mechanical Engineer—'Much can be said in favour of Mr Baker and it is with very real regret that we find ourselves unable, for the reasons indicated, to acquit him of a degree of blame.' (Davies 1967: 97)

> On the Area Mechanical Engineer—'All things considered, and although he is doubtless a good, overworked and conscientious man, Mr Roberts must shoulder a heavy proportion of the blame for its occurrence.' (Davies 1967: 99)

Despite judging the NCB culpable for its lack of policy, individual responsibility focused on those at middle layers within the organisation, not those at the top. When the inquiry report was presented to Parliament, Plaid Cymru MP, Gwynfor Evans, questioned the lack of accountability held by public boards:

> If one drives a car dangerously and has the terrible misfortune to hurt somebody, or perhaps kill somebody, proceedings can be instituted. It is possible for a driver to be convicted of manslaughter. But it is not possible to take

> any sort of action against a public board. There seems to be one law for the private person and another for the public board. I am not suggesting that action should be taken against personal members of the Coal Board. But there should be some way of bringing a public board to justice … If Lord Robens and the Board were responsible for the ultimate direction, surely they are ultimately responsible for what happened. Somebody must be ultimately responsible. (Gwynfor Evans MP, *Hansard*: House of Commons debate on Aberfan inquiry report, 26th October 1967)

MacLean and Johnes (2000) reviewed documents on the Aberfan disaster made available since the inquiry, including disclosure of government papers. Although the disaster occurred before the criminalisation of some relevant offences, civil actions might have been taken as corporations exist as separate legal entities, and vicarious liability of employers for actions of their employees was well established. MacLean and Johnes locate the conclusions of the inquiry, and the lack of any legal proceedings, within the social and political context of Britain in the 1960s. 'The failure to hold anyone accountable for the Aberfan disaster derives from the corporatist assumptions that pervaded British politics at the time … Aberfan was a small working-class community isolated from the heart of UK politics … In corporatist Britain the interests of a nationalised industry took precedence over those of the consumers or the public' (MacLean and Johnes 2000: 220–224).

At issue here is also what has been described as the problem of 'many hands': 'Because many different officials contribute in many ways to decisions and policies of government it is difficult even in principle to identify who is morally responsible for political outcomes. This is what I call the problem of many hands' (Thompson 1980: 905). It lies at the heart of many conflicts over the apportioning of responsibility and blame. 'For outsiders who want to hold functionaries to account regarding the policy or conduct of a complex organisation, it is particularly difficult, and often impossible, to find any person who can be said independently and by his or her own hands to have formed and carried out the policy' (Bovens 1998: 46). Resulting in the 'fragmentation of accountability', where no-one accepts ultimate responsibility, when failures occur, questions are left unanswered. Bovens notes, 'The tangled character of many complex organisations also has an important *moral* dimension. I am referring to the reduction of collective action to individual behaviour … Moral collective responsibilities always end up being imputed to individuals' (Bovens 1998:

110–111). Here there is a contrast with the Aberfan inquiry, where personal responsibility was judged blameworthy, but subordinate to corporate shortcomings, despite the latter escaping sanctions. Half a century on, as dominant discourses give greater weight to personal responsibility, new difficulties emerge in the analysis of culpability. Thompson returned to a discussion on the problem of 'many hands' in a 2014 article reviewing experiences of several major US disasters, including the destruction of New York's World Trade Centre on 9th September 2001 and the deaths of nearly 3000 people. The horrific event led to the setting-up of a ten-member commission to investigate possible failures of government and make recommendations for the future. The subsequent 567-page report 'presented a riveting narrative of the policies and events leading up to the attacks, detailed descriptions of the government's response, and a set of recommendations for changes in the practices and organization of many agencies of government' (Thompson 2014: 4). However, criticisms were levelled at the report for having 'failed to hold any individual accountable; it declined to pass judgment on individuals who made the key decisions ... The Commission's decision to avoid singling out individuals was deliberate: 'Our aim has not been to assign individual blame.' Later, one of the co-chairs explained more fully: '... if we had come up with a list of bad actors, it would have blown the commission apart and it would have blown any credibility we had'' (Thompson 2014: 4).

Thompson's view is that individuals may make mistakes within a context of 'structural defects over which they had no control' (Thompson 2014: 5), but unless analysis of organisational failures includes the details of how decisions were arrived at, there is no real way of knowing what lessons are to be learned. And, he insists, this must include identifying individuals. 'We need to know who did what, not to ascribe blame or mete out punishment, but to guide the design of the roles and organizational culture to prevent future failures—including failures of responsibility' (Thompson 2014: 5). Describing this as a 'modified individualist approach', Thompson argues this is required to acknowledge that failures in complex organisations 'are usually the result of decisions and non-decisions by many different individuals, many of whose contributions may be minimal and unintended'. This should not obviate rights of citizens to hold those responsible to account. 'This individualist approach is necessary even if the purpose is not to punish or discipline individuals but to make changes in the organization to reduce the chances of adverse outcomes in the future' (Thompson 2014: 9). In providing a more informed analysis, this would assist, he believes, in improving the design of institutions. Ultimately, there is a need 'to find ways to strengthen individual responsibility in government and hold its officials accountable to democratic citizens' (Thompson 2014: 10).

Difficulties in disentangling individual and collective failings are paralleled in routes for legal remedy. In the UK until 2007, the common law offence of gross negligence manslaughter, applying to companies and other incorporated bodies, required a senior individual within the organisation (referred to as 'the controlling mind') to be guilty of gross negligence. Under this common law offence, 'the legal test of identification required identifying a company's acts and omissions with those of one or more controlling minds, corporate guilt being dependent on the provable guilt of one or more senior individuals' (the identification principle) (Tombs 2018: 489). However, difficulties in establishing this were illustrated in the case of the P&O ferry company, owners of *Herald of Free Enterprise* which capsized after leaving Zeebrugge on 6 March 1987, with the loss of 193 passengers and crew. In action taken for gross negligence manslaughter, the judge instructed the jury to acquit the company, because the various acts of negligence could not be attributed to a 'controlling mind'. 'Despite the obvious failures of the company, the law simply did not allow the failures of individuals to be aggregated into criminal responsibility by their employer' (Maclean and Johnes 2000: 43). The first successful prosecution of a company followed the drowning in March 1993 of four teenagers from Southway Community College in Plymouth. They had been canoeing in Lyme Bay with four colleagues and a teacher on a trip organised by an outdoors adventure company, OLL Ltd. The company was a small organisation, and the identification of 'the controlling mind' was consequently more straightforward than within a large organisation.

The Corporate Manslaughter and Corporate Homicide Act 2007 (CMCHA) was intended to address what Tombs describes as the 'unjust irony' that made it harder to apply the law to larger and more complex organisations where the 'identification principle' is more difficult to apply. Under the new legislation, the central test of guilt would be to establish 'a failure in the way in which the organization was managed or organized which amounted to a gross breach of the duty of care'. Removing the identification principle 'by establishing the *senior management* test', this required evidence of failure at senior management level, 'but it was not necessary to identify specific individuals, nor indeed, their specific failures which contributed to the death' (Tombs 2018: 491). But in terms of the impact of the legislation, Tombs notes an apparent paradox, with the 'senior management' test being an issue in only one case out of twenty-one successful prosecutions and three acquittals under the Act. Suggesting the others could almost certainly have been prosecuted under the common law offence of manslaughter, Tombs argues:

> If, then, *corporate* accountability has not been improved in the implementation of the new law thus far, we have also seen clear indications that in the abandonment of the identification principle, ***individual*** liability for gross negligence deaths at work appears to have been reduced – with liability being transferred from individuals to the corporate entity. In this exchange, the corporate veil, itself a key source of corporate negligence, has been reinforced. (Tombs 2018: 504–505, emphasis in original)

Individual blame may unfairly apportion responsibility, but systemic explanations risk substituting this with no-one being accountable because everyone is responsible. This dilemma parallels the contrast of dispositional and situational explanations in attribution theory, and in what Dawe described as 'two sociologies': 'a sociology of social system and a sociology of social action … One views action as the derivative of system, whilst the other views system as the derivative of action' (Dawe 1970: 214). Although Dawe contends 'that sociology has developed on the basis of the conflict between them', as with the public/private boundary, and system/people contrasts, these are not binary opposites. The identification of responsibility when things go wrong requires transparency, but this can be at odds with claims for individual autonomy and privacy. Social values and the emergence of a legal framework around privacy and transparency provide the focus for the following chapter.

References

Assinder, N. (1999, July 7). Blair Risks Row Over Public Sector. *BBC News*. http://news.bbc.co.uk/1/hi/uk_politics/388528.stm

Bailey, J. (2000). Some Meanings of "The Private" in Sociological Thought. *Sociology, 34*(3), 381–401.

Bourdieu, P. (1989). Social Space and Symbolic Power. *Sociological Theory, 7*(1), 14–25.

Bovens, M. (1998). *The Quest for Responsibility: Accountability and Citizenship in Complex Organisations*. Cambridge: Cambridge University Press.

Brewer, J. (2005). The Public and Private in C. Wright Mills's Life and Work. *Sociology, 39*(4), 661–677.

Camdessus, M. (1997, November 13). *Lessons from Southeast Asia*. Singapore: International Monetary Fund Press Briefing.

Davies, Sir H. E. (Chairman) (1967). *Report of the Tribunal Appointed to Inquire into the Disaster at Aberfan on October 21st, 1966*. London: Her Majesty's Stationery Office. http://www.mineaccidents.com.au/uploads/aberfan-report-original.pdf)

Davies, W. (2015). The Chronic Social: Relations of Control Within and Without Neoliberalism. *New Formations: A Journal of Culture/Theory Politics, 84*(85), 40–57.

Dawe, A. (1970). The Two Sociologies. *British Journal of Sociology, 21*, 207–218.

Deleuze, G. (1992, October). Postscript on Societies of Control. *October, 59*, 3–7.

Durkheim, E. (1893/1997). *The Division of Labour in Society*. New York: Free Press.

Etzioni, A. (2010). Is Transparency the Best Disinfectant? *The Journal of Political Philosophy, 18*(4), 389–404.

Foucault, M. (1980). The Eye of Power. In C. Gordon (Ed.), *Power/Knowledge: Selected Interviews and Other Writings* (pp. 1972–1977). New York: Pantheon Books.

Goffman, E. (1972). *Relations in Public: Microstudies of the Social Order*. Harmondsworth: Penguin.

HM Government. (2010). *The Coalition: Our Programme for Government*. London: Cabinet Office.

Holmes, M. (2000). When Is the Personal Political? The President's Penis and Other Stories. *Sociology, 34*(2), 305–321.

Lemke. (2001). 'The Birth of Bio-Politics': Michel Foucault's Lecture at the Collège de France on Neo-Liberal Governmentality. *Economy and Society, 30*(2), 190–207.

Maclean, I., & Johnes, M. (2000). *Aberfan: Government and Disasters*. Cardiff: Welsh Academic Press.

McGuigan, J. (2014). The Neoliberal Self. *Culture Unbound, 6*, 223–240.

McNay, L. (2009). Self as Enterprise: Dilemmas of Control and Resistance in Foucault's the Birth of Biopolitics. *Theory, Culture and Society, 26*(6), 55–77.

Meijer, A. (2014). Transparency. In M. Bovens, R. E. Goodin, & T. Schillemans (Eds.), *The Oxford Handbook of Public Accountability* (pp. 507–524). Oxford: Oxford University Press.

Mill, J. S., & Lerner, M. (1965). *Essential Works of John Stuart Mill*. New York: Bantam Books.

Moore, S. (2018). Towards a Sociology of Institutional Transparency: Openness, Deception and the Problem of Public Trust. *Sociology, 52*(2), 416–430.

Morgan, G. (1986). *Images of Organization*. Beverley Hills: Sage.

Pateman, C. (1989). *The Disorder of Women: Democracy, Feminism and Political Theory*. Cambridge: Polity Press.
Perrow, C. (1999). *Normal Accidents: Living with High Risk Technologies*. Princeton: Princeton University Press.
Peters, M. (2001). Education, Enterprise Culture and the Entrepreneurial Self: A Foucauldian Perspective. *Journal of Educational Enquiry, 2*(2), 58–71.
Power, M. (1999). *The Audit Society: Rituals of Verification*. Oxford: Oxford University Press.
Pyysiainen, J., Halpin, D., & Guilfoyle, A. (2017). Neoliberal Governance and 'Responsibilization' of Agents: Reassessing the Mechanisms of Responsibility-Shift in Neoliberal Discursive Environments. *Distinktion: Journal of Social Theory, 18*(2), 215–235.
Ribbens-McCarthy, J., & Edwards, R. (2001). Illuminating Meanings of "The Private" in Sociological Thought. *Sociology, 35*(3), 765–777.
Rose, N. (1992). Governing the Enterprising Self. In P. Heelas & P. Morris (Eds.), *The Values of the Enterprise Culture: The Moral Debate* (pp. 141–164). London: Routledge.
Rossler, B. (2005). *The Value of Privacy* (R. D. V. Glasgow, Trans.). Cambridge: Polity Press.
Secretary of State for Health. (2006). *Our Health, Our Care, Our Say: A New Direction for Community Services*. London: HMSO.
Seidman, S. (1994). The New Social Movements and the Making of New Social Knowledges. In S. Seidman (Ed.), *Contested Knowledge: Social Theory in the Postmodern Era*. Oxford: Blackwell.
Simonet, D. (2011). The New Public Management Theory and the Reform of European Health Care Systems: An International Comparative Perspective. *International Journal of Public Administration, 34*(12), 815–826.
Thompson, D. F. (1980, December). Moral Responsibility of Public Officials: The Problem of Many Hands. *The American Political Science Review, 74*(4), 905–916A.
Thompson, J. B. (2011). Shifting Boundaries of Public and Private Life. *Theory, Culture and Society, 28*(4), 49–70.
Thompson, D. F. (2014, May). Responsibility for Failures of Government: The Problem of Many Hands. *American Journal of Public Administration, 44*(3), 259–227.
Tombs, S. (2018). The UK's Corporate Killing Law: Un/Fit for Purpose? *Criminology & Criminal Justice, 18*(4), 488–507.
Turner, B. (1976, September). The Organizational and Interorganizational Development of Disasters. *Administrative Science Quarterly, 1*, 378–397.
Vaughan, D. (1990). Autonomy, Interdependence, and Social Control: NASA and the Space Shuttle Challenger. *Administrative Science Quarterly, 35*(2), 225–257.

Vaughan, D. (1996). *The Challenger Launch Decision*. Chicago: University of Chicago Press.
Wacquant, L. (1992). Methodological Relationism. In P. Bourdieu & L. Wacquant (Eds.), *An Invitation to Reflexive Sociology*. Cambridge/Oxford: Polity Press/Blackwell.
Wilensky, H. L. (1967). *Organizational Intelligence*. New York: Basic Books.
Williams, R. (1983). *Keywords: A Vocabulary of Culture and Society*. London: Flamingo Press.
Zerubavel, E. (1997). *Social Mindscapes: An Invitation to Cognitive Sociology*. Cambridge, MA/London: Harvard University Press.

CHAPTER 3

A Right to Privacy and a Right to Know

Abstract Contested boundaries between 'public' and 'private' gain further importance with expanding conceptions of human rights. The guarantee of respect for 'private life' in the European Convention on Human Rights, subsequently developed through European case law to embrace reputation and relationships, provides a context for increasing attention given in the UK to the protection of privacy and personal data. However, conflicts between public and private emerge in counter-claims to freedom of expression and rights to a private life. The development of freedom of information legislation in the UK marked a new departure, but with increasing use of data protection legislation to avoid FOIA disclosure, the House of Commons expenses scandal illustrates further conflicting claims over rights to privacy and freedom of information.

Keywords Human Rights • European Convention on Human Rights • Privacy • Freedom of information • Public interest

Responding to revelations that he claimed £90,000 over four years for the upkeep of his country estate, Anthony Steen MP told the BBC in 2009, 'As far as I'm concerned, and as of this day, I don't know what all the fuss is about. What right does the public have to interfere with my private life? None. Do you know what this reminds me of? An episode of *Coronation Street*' (Lewis 2019). While the MP's expenses scandal deepened public

M. Sheaff, *Secrecy, Privacy and Accountability*,
https://doi.org/10.1007/978-3-030-11686-6_3

mistrust, protection of personal privacy gained increasing attention, much of it generated by concerns about less legitimate media intrusion into private lives. The Levenson Inquiry, established following revelations of telephone hacking by *News of the World* journalists, put the relationship between personal privacy and press freedom under the spotlight. One of the draft criteria for a regulatory solution proposed by the inquiry stated: 'It must recognise the importance for the public interest of a free press in a democracy, freedom of expression and investigative journalism, the rule of law, personal privacy and other private rights, and a press which acts responsibly and in the public interest' (Levenson 2012: Vol. 1, p. 29). As journalism provides the context for many conflicting claims about privacy rights, particularly relating to freedom of expression, examples from this setting are used as a route for considering conflicts over 'public' and 'personal' information.

An important backdrop for much of what follows is the European Convention on Human Rights, for which Andrew Ashworth QC, and Oxford professor of English Law, has described 'three levels of strength of its rights'. The first consists of non-derogable rights, including the right to life, the right not to be subject to torture or inhuman or degrading treatment, and the right not to be subject to forced labour. These, 'must be upheld in all circumstances, no matter how dire the political situation, no matter whether there is a state of war or a "public emergency threatening the life of the nation"'. Secondly, there are 'strong rights', including the right to liberty and security of the person, and the right to a fair trial. The third 'category of Convention rights might be termed qualified or *prima facie* rights—the right is declared, but it is also declared that it may be interfered with on certain grounds, to the minimum extent possible. Examples of this are the right to respect for private life, the right to freedom of thought and the right to freedom of expression, and the right to freedom of assembly and association. All these qualified rights are subject to interference, if it can be established that this is "necessary in a democratic society" on one of the stated grounds' (Ashworth 2002: 75–76).

Writing in 1993, Turner noted a 'silence about rights in sociology', despite the fact that 'contests over rights as claims or entitlements are a major feature of modern social life' (Turner 1993: 490). Turner's view was that a scepticism towards ideas of natural rights in classical sociology resulted in a focus on the sociology of citizenship in its place. Seeking to counter the largely negative view of rights within this tradition, Turner argues that increasing state power and erosion of citizen rights means 'the debate about rights might begin to replace the debate about citizenship in both academic and political life' (Turner 1993: 509). Addressing feminist critiques of the public/private division, Turner acknowledges that 'rights mask underlying structural inequalities by an appeal to the sovereignty of the individual (but) it is wrong to dismiss all versions of rights theory on the grounds that one version is found wanting' (Turner 1993: 507).

Special sociological significance of this lies in the capacity for what Ashworth described as 'third-tier' rights to create a site for conflict and accommodation. This chapter includes detail on a number of cases where some of these issues were in dispute. The purpose is not to provide a legal commentary, but to illustrate something of the changing socio-legal context to set the scene for issues considered in Chap. 4 on studying state institutions.

A Right to Privacy?

Privacy has been described as the 'claim of individuals, groups or institutions to determine for themselves when, how, and to what extent information about them is communicated to others' (Westin 1967: 7). Typically regarded as being of benefit to the individual, providing a private space protected from the gaze of others, several writers also emphasise the social value of privacy. It has been described as 'a bulwark against totalitarianism ... vital for democracy' (Hughes 2015: 228), and 'essential to democratic government because it fosters and encourages the moral autonomy of the citizen, a central requirement of a democracy' (Gavison 1980: 455). 'One of the core values of privacy is that it allows individuals to have distance from the state: no democracy can flourish where individuals have no privacy from the state' (Hughes 2015: 229). Similarly, describing privacy as a 'fundamental requirement' for democracy, Lever suggests 'people are entitled to keep some true facts about themselves to themselves, should they so wish, as a sign of respect for their moral and political status, and in order to protect themselves from being used as a public example in order to educate or entertain other people' (Lever 2015: 163).

Liberal approaches to privacy regard it as akin to a property right (Mill and Lerner 1965: 232), while communitarian critics have charged liberalism with what Macpherson described as 'possessive individualism', having a 'conception of the individual as essentially the proprietor of his own person or capacities, owing nothing to society for them' (Macpherson 1962: 3). A somewhat similar concern is expressed by Etzioni (in the context of the USA), who argues, 'laws limiting the right of the press to report on the scandalous behavior of public officials, corporate executives, foundation officials and others, or which make it too easy to win libel suits against other citizens, not only raise First Amendment concerns, but also may extend privacy too far, diminishing communal scrutiny and undermining the common good' (Etzioni 2000: 905).

Fuchs (2011) similarly raises objections to giving primacy to privacy rights. He provides a summary of criticisms of privacy laws for potentially allowing deception, harming the public and common good, concealing and even legitimising domestic violence, and facilitating the planning and commission of illegal or antisocial activities. 'These critiques show that the question is therefore not how privacy can be best protected, but in which cases whose privacy should be protected and in which cases it should not be protected' (Fuchs 2011: 225). A very different view was taken by Edward Shils half a century ago, who regarded 'intrusions on privacy' as 'baneful because they interfere with an individual in his disposition of what belongs to him' (Shils 1966: 306). However, he drew a distinction between 'personal privacy'—including 'relationships of personal affinity and hostility, of friendship and love and hatred, erotic relationships or practices, the primordial relationship of spouses, of parents and children, of siblings, of kinsmen, and of neighbours' (Shils 1966: 283)—and 'corporate privacy'. The latter involved 'conversations about corporate actions, conversations about competitive educational and occupational performances in corporate bodies, conversations about public matters may all occur in the private sphere … But despite their context, they are not personal private matters in our sense' (Shils 1966: 283–284).

Academic discussions on the privacy of office holders are limited, tending to focus on the protection of the private lives of officials from scrutiny, rather than the creation of private spaces for their deliberations. One example is Holmes's (2000) discussion on Paula Jones, a former Arkansas state employee who sued President Bill Clinton for sexual harassment. He denied the claim, but agreed an out-of-court settlement of $850,000. Holmes describes how:

> the majority of citizens, according to opinion polls, generally seemed to think his sexual behaviour was a 'personal' issue. What has emerged is weariness with hearing about what the president does or does not do with his penis. 'So what?' people say and they may in many ways be right. However, considerable suffering has resulted from his supposedly 'personal' actions and women are the primary sufferers. (Holmes 2000: 316)

Nearly two decades on, the #MeToo movement drew renewed attention to the personal/public boundary in the particular context of sexual harassment, but attitudes to what should be disclosed here and more broadly remain complex. A review of work in this field, mainly from normative political philosophy, identifies a prevailing view as being 'citizens are entitled to know about those personal matters of office holders that are relevant for assessing their (past or likely future) performance in office. Accessibility of such information is a condition of the political accountability of government officials' (Mokrosinska 2015: 182). Asking the question 'are the private affairs of public officials a matter of public concern?', Mokrosinska considers whether holders of public office are expected 'to display character traits that align with a set of politically correct values also in their private conduct ... do probity or failings in personal life portend probity or failings in office' (Mokrosinska 2015: 181–182). Noting research evidence suggesting 'there is no convincing evidence either way' on this (see Thompson 2005), Mokrosinska rejects the view that obtaining full information about candidates makes the right to vote more meaningful. Although analogous to the idea of the informed consumer, Mokrosinska contends 'the renouncement of the privacy of office holders undermines the liberal-democratic commitments to equality and freedom rather than aligns with them' (Mokrosinska 2015: 183). Lever makes a similar point:

> people have important personal and political interests in confidentiality, which are intimately related to democratic ideas about the way power should be distributed, used and justified in a society ... they are not in need of constant hectoring or supervision in order to act well, although they are rightly accountable to appropriate public authorities for their exercise of public powers, their use of public resources and their respect for others' rights. (Lever 2015: 178)

Mokrosinska refers to a suggestion by Nagel (1998) that 'the public-private boundary keeps the public domain free of disruptive material', with the latter potentially including information about sexual affairs, private racism, sexism, homophobia, religious and ethnic bigotry, sexual puritanism 'and other such private pleasures' (Nagel 1998: 30). But these examples again serve to illustrate 'the slippery nature of the distinction between the public and the private' (Etzioni 2000: 899). 'Private' views on racism, sexism, homophobia and bigotry held by public officials might also be judged as public issues. Recognising difficulties in establishing absolute rules in such circumstances, Mokrosinska concludes that the defining criteria should be public justification. 'In sorting out which material is appropriate and inappropriate for individuals to introduce into the political forum, public justification sets out rules of concealment and disclosure between individuals acting in their political capacity' (Mokrosinska 2015: 187). She develops this to argue the contribution of normative consensus in the construction of these boundaries:

> The border between the political and the private is constructed out of reasons that people can and cannot reasonably accept as governing their life together; that is, reasons that meet and fail to meet the test of public justification. Public justification sorts out the material that falls in and out of the political realm. Failures to provide reasons that others can reasonably accept therefore identify the material that counts as private from the perspective of liberal politics. (Mokrosinska 2015: 188)

While questions of public justification have been to the fore in the development of privacy rights, given the contested character of the private-public divide, these become most acute when challenged by counterveiling rights, notably those of freedom of expression. Privacy debates emerged later in the UK than in the USA, possibly attributable to a stronger normative acceptance of privacy and secrecy in Britain (Shils 1956). Warren and Brandeis, said to have 'invented the right to privacy in the context of late nineteenth century America' (Glancy 1979: 38–39), believed that 'political, social, and economic changes entail the recognition of new rights', highlighting excessive intrusion by newspapers:

> The press is overstepping in every direction the obvious bounds of propriety and of decency ... The intensity and complexity of life, attendant upon advancing civilization, have rendered necessary some retreat from the world, and man, under the refining influence of culture, has become more sensitive to publicity, so that solitude and privacy have become more essential to the individual; but modern enterprise and invention have, through invasions upon his privacy, subjected him to mental pain and distress, far greater than could be inflicted by mere bodily injury. (Warren and Brandeis 1890: 196)

Shils attributes the early emergence of privacy as an issue in the USA rather than in the UK to the former's founding commitment to openness and the latter's tradition of secrecy. 'The United States has been committed to the principle of publicity since its origin. The atmosphere of distrust of aristocracy in which the American Republic spent its formative years has persisted in many forms. Repugnance for governmental secretiveness was an offspring of the distrust of aristocracy' (Shils 1956: 215). In contrast, 'the acceptance of hierarchy in British society permits the government to retain its secrets, with little challenge or resentment' (Shils 1956: 218). Deference and a 'feeling of affinity which members of the elite in Great Britain have toward one another' increased the acceptability of secrecy (Shils 1956: 219). The UK Justice Committee's *Privacy and the Law* concluded in 1970 that while there was a 'strong case' for establishing a right to privacy, it was reluctant to provide a definition of precisely what this covered. Instead, the report explained 'we shall use the word "privacy" in the report in the sense of that area of a man's life which, in any given circumstances, a reasonable man with an understanding of the legitimate needs of the community would think it wrong to invade' (Cited in Gavison 1980: 426). Examples of circumstances which might be embraced by this description included the unauthorised recording of conversations, taking of visual images or copying of documents.

The subsequent Committee on Privacy, chaired by Sir Kenneth Younger, considered 'whether legislation is needed to give further protection to the privacy of individuals and companies against intrusions from other individuals and companies', deciding by a majority of fourteen to two not to recommend such a right. In its report, the Committee explained it felt 'unable to devise any satisfactory yardstick by which to judge, in cases of doubt, whether the importance of a public story should override the privacy of the people and personal information involved' (Younger 1973: para 187). One member of the Committee expanded on this: 'The first difficulty we faced as a Committee was in trying to define "privacy", and in the event we decided that it could not satisfactorily be done. We looked at many earlier attempts, and we noted that they either went very wide, equating the right to privacy with the right to be let alone, or that they amounted to a catalogue of assorted values to which the adjectives "private" or "personal" could reasonably be applied. In the Report we list the various definitions which have been attempted in the past; but, as I have said, we did not attempt a definition ourselves' (Lord Byers, *Hansard*, HL Debate 06 June 1973, vol 343 c106). Providing the government's provisional response to the report, the Home Secretary, Robert Carr, told the House of Commons: 'privacy is important. It is something which at different times we all need and its presence or absence is a useful measure of the quality of life in our society. A society which attaches importance to privacy is almost by definition a society which also attaches importance to the individual generally'. But Carr noted, 'Inevitably the issue becomes a conflict between the right of the individual to keep his affairs private and the right of others to speak or write of them freely, and particularly to speak and write things which are true and arguably of public importance' (Carr, *Hansard*, HC 13 July 1973). He continued:

> Unlike many other countries, we do not have a written constitution, and the creation of general rights is not the way in which our law has traditionally sought to protect fundamental human freedoms. Freedom of speech, freedom of conscience, the right of free assembly are not in any way guaranteed by statute in this country ... I simply do not believe that in these matters ... there is some absolute objective truth, some absolute objective right point. All we can do at any given moment is to try to strike a balance between these inevitable conflicts of interest. (Carr, *Hansard* HC 13 July 1973)

During the debate, Labour shadow minister Shirley Williams pointed out, 'It is also worth underlining that the Government have subscribed to two major declarations on the right to privacy. I refer to the United Nations Convention on Human Rights and to the European Convention on Human Rights, Article 8, which sets out clearly: "Everyone has the right to respect of his private and family life, his home and his correspondence"'. She went on to consider the 'balance between a general right of privacy and the rights of the Press and others to investigate matters which they believe to be of importance to society ... I am also persuaded that no general right of privacy could be conceded without an absolute defence of public interest for newspapers, for the BBC and for television, because investigative journalism is a crucial part of the safeguards that we need in our type of society' (Williams, *Hansard* HC 13 July 1973). Another Labour member, David Owen MP, took a different view: 'myself and other hon. Members, particularly hon. Members on this side, are advocating in many areas an extension of community politics—an emphasis on the community. We must face the fact that the community and reduced privacy in some ways go hand in hand' (Owen, *Hansard* HC 13 July 1973).

The balance between media intrusion and investigative journalism was prominent in subsequent developments. A notable case involved journalists working for the *Sunday Sport* posing as doctors to take photographs of actor Gordon Kaye recovering in hospital from head injuries. Hit by a piece of advertising hoarding that smashed through his car windscreen during the storms of January 1990, Kaye was subjected to what an Appeal Court judge described as a 'monstrous invasion of privacy'. Lord Justice Glidewell added, 'It is well known that in English law there is no right to privacy, and accordingly there is no right of action for breach of a person's privacy. The facts of the present case are a graphic illustration of the desirability of Parliament considering whether and in what circumstances statutory provision can be made to protect the privacy of individuals' (Glidewell LJ in *Kaye v Robertson & Sports Newspapers Ltd. 1991*). Although the UK was a signatory to Article 8 of the European Convention on Human Rights, this was not embodied in UK legislation until the 1998 Human Rights Act. Article 8 does not use the word privacy, although the word does appear in Article 12 of the Universal Declaration of Human Rights, which Article 8 was ostensibly designed to implement. In full, Article 8 states:

1. *Everyone has the right to respect for his private and family life, his home and his correspondence.*
2. *There shall be no interference by a public authority with the exercise of this right except such as is in accordance with the law and is necessary in a democratic society in the interests of national security, public safety or the economic well-being of the country, for the prevention of disorder or crime, for the protection of health or morals, or for the protection of the rights and freedoms of others.*

Rights to freedom of expression are guaranteed by Article 10 of the European Convention, which states:

1. *Everyone has the right to freedom of expression. This right shall include freedom to hold opinions and to receive and impart information and ideas without interference by public authority and regardless of frontiers. This Article shall not prevent States from requiring the licensing of broadcasting, television or cinema enterprises.*
2. *The exercise of these freedoms, since it carries with it duties and responsibilities, may be subject to such formalities, conditions, restrictions or penalties as are prescribed by law and are necessary in a democratic society, in the interests of national security, territorial integrity or public safety, for the prevention of disorder or crime, for the protection of health or morals, for the protection of the reputation or rights of others, for preventing the disclosure of information received in confidence, or for maintaining the authority and impartiality of the judiciary.*

Conflicting approaches of liberal and communitarian writers are reflected in an observation by Hughes (2015) on decisions by the European Court of Human Rights when considering the balance between Articles 8 and 10. Hughes suggests that when considering Article 8, the Court's focus has been upon benefits to the individual, whereas the Court emphasises benefits to society when considering Article 9 (Freedom of thought, conscience and religion), Article 10 (Freedom of expression) and Article 11 (Freedom of assembly and association). Further, in assessing the balance between conflicting rights, the European Court has adopted a broad view of what is 'private', as illustrated in an early judgment:

> The Court does not consider it possible or necessary to attempt an exhaustive definition of the notion of "private life". However, it would be too restrictive to limit the notion to an "inner circle" in which the individual may live his own personal life as he chooses and to exclude therefrom entirely the outside world not encompassed within that circle. Respect for private life must also comprise to a certain degree the right to establish and develop relationships with other human beings. There appears, furthermore, to be no reason of principle why this understanding of the notion of "private life" should be taken to exclude activities of a professional or business nature since it is, after all, in the course of their working lives that the majority of people have a significant, if not the greatest, opportunity of developing relationships with the outside world. (*Niemietz v. Germany* 1992)

In the context of this approach, subsequent cases have developed reasoning on the implications for personal reputation. In one such case, heard in 2006, the applicant claimed Swedish Courts had not given protection from damaging newspaper allegations that he had involvement in serious criminal activities, including the 1986 murder of the Prime Minister, Olaf Palme. The Court acknowledged, 'the statements clearly tarnished his reputation and, moreover, disregarded his right to be presumed innocent until proven guilty according to law' (para 25), but concluded: 'the public interest in publishing the information in question outweighed the applicant's right to the protection of his reputation. Consequently, the Court cannot find that there has been a failure on the part of the Swedish State to afford adequate protection of the applicant's rights under Article 8 of the Convention' (*White v Sweden* 2006: para 30).

In other cases, a perceived lack of evidence to substantiate statements led to different outcomes. One concerned the suicide of an Austrian professor who had launched unsuccessful defamation proceedings after being accused of dismissing the enormity of Nazi crimes and suggesting Jews had invaded Germany. Following the suicide, the author of these claims was subject to allegations he had caused the professor's death, causing him to initiate his own proceedings alleging defamation. These too were unsuccessful, and the applicant claimed the Austrian Courts had failed to protect his right to reputation under Article 8. The majority decision of the European Court was that as the allegation against him was not substantiated, his rights to privacy had indeed been violated: 'a person's reputation, even if that person is criticised in the context of a public debate, forms part of his or her personal identity and psychological integrity and therefore also falls within the scope of his or her "private life"' (*Pfeifer v Austria* 2007).

Another case concerned a novel entitled *Jean-Marie le Pen on Trial*, based on real events, including murders of two young men for which members of the Front National were convicted. Although fictionalised, the novel contains several statements about M Le Pen, such as the question, 'isn't the chairman of the Front National responsible for the murder committed by one of his teenage militants inflamed by his rhetoric?' After being convicted of defamation by the French courts, the case went to the European Court which determined that rights to freedom of expression also involve 'duties and responsibilities', particularly where real people are referred to. While accepting that M Le Pen had convictions for racial hatred, the Court maintained he was entitled to the protection afforded by Article 8. Judge Loucaides emphasised that the right to reputation is 'part and parcel of the right to respect for one's private life' and is in consequence 'an autonomous human right, which derives its source from the Convention itself'. He went on to describe reputation as 'a sacred value for every person including politicians and is safeguarded as a human right under the Convention for the benefit of every individual without exception' (*Lindon, Otchakovsky-Laurens and July v France* 2007).

The balance between rights to privacy and protection of reputation, and freedom of expression came to the fore in Britain in the summer of 2018 in legal proceedings taken by Sir Cliff Richard against the BBC and South Yorkshire Police (SYP). The action, resulting in awards of £230,000 damages and £190,000 costs against the BBC by the High Court in July 2018, arose from news reports of an allegation of an historic sex offence made against Sir Cliff. A BBC reporter, having learned of an investigation by SYP into the allegation from a confidential source, arranged a meeting with SYP's media officer and an SYP superintendent. At the meeting, the reporter was told of an intention to search Sir Cliff's home in Berkshire.

The subsequent search received 'prominent and extensive television coverage' by the BBC (Judgment, para 2). Sir Cliff's home was in a locked, gated complex, and the BBC used a helicopter to provide film footage as the search was underway.

Sir Cliff was not arrested, and no charges were brought against him. Having settled a claim with SYP, he continued action against the BBC for violating his privacy, to which the BBC responded with a defence based on Article 10. The High Court judgment pointed out, 'where the two rights potentially conflict the court has to carry out a balancing exercise between those rights' (*Sir Cliff Richard OBE and The British Broadcasting Corporation & The Chief Constable of South Yorkshire Police 2018: para 229*). On sharing information about a police investigation, the judge ruled 'a suspect has a reasonable expectation of privacy in relation to a police investigation ... (because) of the stigma attached'. The judge continued:

> If the presumption of innocence were perfectly understood and given effect to, and if the general public was universally capable of adopting a completely open- and broad-minded view of the fact of an investigation so that there was no risk of taint either during the investigation or afterwards (assuming no charge) then the position might be different. But neither of those things is true. The fact of an investigation, as a general rule, will of itself carry some stigma, no matter how often one says it should not. (para 248)

Adding he was not suggesting 'an invariable right to privacy' (para 251), Mr Justice Mann addressed the BBC's defence that it was a legitimate matter of public interest as Sir Cliff was a public figure:

> A public figure is not, by virtue of that quality, necessarily deprived of his or her legitimate expectations of privacy ... It may be that a given public figure waives at least a degree of privacy by courting publicity, or adopting a public stance which would be at odds with the privacy rights claimed, but nothing like that applies in the present case. (para 256)

Later he added, 'it does not follow that, because an investigation at a general level was a matter of public interest, the identity of the subject of the investigation also attracted that characterisation' (para 282). Describing the balancing of rights as 'an overall evaluative exercise which is not a precise scientific measuring one' (para 315), factors given particular attention were the 'very, very serious' consequences for Sir Cliff in the context of the 'stigma attached to the revelation' (para 316).

The judgment met a mostly hostile media response, particularly from columnists:

After Cliff Richard's victory, the BBC must fight back to preserve justice… and a free press (*The Sun*, 20 July 2018).
Cliff Richard v BBC has set a terrible precedent—the media must fight back (*The Guardian*, 22 July 2018).
Congratulations, Sir Cliff—you've just done sex offenders a big favour (*The Herald*, Scotland, 22 July 2018).

In contrast, a YouGov poll on 19 and 20 July 2018 found 'overwhelming public support for pre-charge anonymity of suspects', with 86% of respondents supporting anonymity for suspects under investigation and 83% supporting the anonymity of those arrested. YouGov commented, 'the poll results show that the public has not been convinced by the one sided media coverage of the Cliff Richard judgment' (YouGov 2018). Public opinion appears to have been shaped by a view that the BBC's reporting of the allegations was at least premature, and unjustified given that he had no charges laid against him and nor was he even arrested. It was not seen as an example of investigative journalism so much as an unacceptable intrusion into privacy and an unjustified threat to Sir Cliff's reputation. But another high-profile privacy issue in the summer of 2018 suggests public attitudes on privacy can be balanced by other concerns. Use of personal data by the political consulting firm Cambridge Analytica (CA) brought to the fore intrusion into the privacy of those, not in the public eye, but simply making use of social media.

In July 2018, the Information Commissioner published reports into the use of data analytics in political campaigns (Information Commissioner 2018a), and on personal information and political influence (ICO 2018b). The ICO investigation was prompted by reports in *The Observer* newspaper that during the EU referendum campaign, CA provided data to the Leave.UK campaign that supported micro-targeting of voters. Its focus was the 'complex eco-system that exists between data brokerage organisations, social media platforms and political campaigns and parties' (ICO 2018b: 9). A key strand of the investigation concerned an app developed by Global Science Research (GSR), the origins of which lay in research carried out by the Psychometric Centre at the University of Cambridge since 2005. This included use of the 'five-factor' model of personality (Digman 1990), which suggests five domains explain most individual differences in personality, these being: Openness to experience, Conscientiousness, Extraversion, Agreeableness and Neuroticism (sometimes described by its acronym as the OCEAN model). Results from 'My Personality', an app developed by the Cambridge Centre in 2013, allowed users' OCEAN scores to be matched with other online data, including Facebook posts, 'likes' and shares. It was claimed a review of 68 'likes' by a person on Facebook allowed a prediction 'with a high degree of accuracy' of a number of characteristics and traits, as well as ethnicity and political affiliation.

The app was developed as a commercial venture, through GSR, which entered into an agreement with the parent company of CA. Data were harvested from Facebook on an industrial scale. This included data of 1 million people in the UK, and at least 50 million people globally—Facebook estimated the total number might be 87 million (ICO 2018a: 16). Announcing an intention to fine Facebook £500,000, the Information Commissioner, Elizabeth Denham, said 'Facebook has failed to provide the kind of protections they are required to under the Data Protection Act ... Fines and prosecutions punish the bad actors, but my real goal is to effect change and restore trust and confidence in our democratic system' (Hern and Pegg 2018). The episode brought to life comments by Latour in a 2007 article, 'Beware Your Imagination Leaves Digital Traces': 'It is as if the inner workings of private worlds have been pried open because their inputs and outputs have become thoroughly traceable' (Latour 2007: 2). There are questions about whether 'big data' really can provide the sort of insights that CA and others claim (for earlier discussions, see for example Manovich 2011, and Halford 2015), but that aside, opinion poll evidence suggests considerable—but not unanimous—public support for the ICO's stance. In a survey conducted by BMG for *The Independent* newspaper in April 2018, '60 per cent of respondents either "strongly" supported or "somewhat" supported the statement that Facebook should now be fined by the government over the revelations ... Just 10 per cent of those polled opposed sanctioning the company while 21 per cent said neither support nor oppose and a further 9 per cent replied, "don't know". Similar results were reflected across all age groups' (Cowburn 2018).

However, an earlier YouGov survey, conducted in February 2017, points to some important nuances in public attitudes towards the protection of personal digital data. When asked what most concerned them, 39% referred to 'companies collecting and sharing your personal data online with other organisations', compared to 66% mentioning cyber-crime and 46% cyber-attacks. Only 21% identified 'online surveillance of UK citizens by the UK Government' as an issue they were most concerned about. Protection of personal information is not considered an absolute principle or right. Similarly, just 26% wanted more done to protect privacy even if this limits government's ability to fight crime or protect national security. For Conservative voters, this fell to 16% (Rogers de Waal 2017).

Opinion polls can be uncertain indicators, particularly on issues such as privacy and surveillance for which the impact of events, including terrorist outrages as well as corporate or media abuses, can stimulate rapidly changing moods. The responses nevertheless reflect notions of justifiability in the construction of boundaries for the protection of privacy. Over the past four decades, Britain has witnessed enormous changes in the cultural, legal and political status of privacy, but something remains of previous attitudes and values resisting an absolutist approach. Legal protections are not ineluctable. Case law, public opinion and scholarly debate all provide support for the defence of privacy, while acknowledging circumstances where its protection may be legitimately outweighed by other principles. Much attention has focused on conflicts with freedom of expression, but issues also arise in relation to broader objectives of transparency, and specifically the introduction of freedom of information legislation.

Privacy and a Right to Information?

After the introduction of the US Freedom of Information Act in 1966, several unsuccessful attempts were made to secure similar legislation in the UK through private members' bills. A commitment to pass such legislation made by Labour in 1974 was not fulfilled, but was repeated in the party's 1997 manifesto. This stated: 'Unnecessary secrecy in government leads to arrogance in government and defective policy decisions ... We are pledged to a Freedom of Information Act, leading to more open government'. Publication of the *Your Right to Know* White Paper in 1998 led the Canadian Information Commissioner to write, 'Canada's once brave, state-of-the-art Access to Information Act is being left behind by Britain ... (the White Paper) represents nothing other than a breath-taking transformation in the relationship between the government and the governed' (Information Commissioner of Canada 1998). But the subsequent Bill met widespread disappointment from freedom of information supporters. Hugo Young, political correspondent of *The Guardian*, wrote: The Freedom of Information Bill marks its definitive transition from a party dedicated to changing the world, into a government determined its own world shall not be changed. The purpose of this reform, as canvassed in opposition, was to alter the balance of power between citizen and state … The Bill now disgorged is a spectacular betrayal of any such idea (Young 1999).

Important changes were secured during parliamentary passage of the Bill, including establishing a role for the Information Commissioner to order disclosure when justified in the public interest, and considerable limitations were imposed on the use of vetoes. While not as path-breaking as first anticipated, the Act nonetheless created a route for accessing information going considerably beyond anything previously available. When it came into effect, there were twenty-two exemptions, with five of particular relevance to concepts of secrecy, framed below within Shils (1966) distinction between personal and corporate privacy. Table 3.1 shows the percentage of all refusals by UK central government-monitored bodies falling within each of these exemptions, for 2005 and 2017.

Since 2005 there has been a fall in the proportion of all exemptions coming within these five categories from 74.3% to 68.8%, but the more notable shift is in the balance between those described here as 'personal' and 'corporate' privacy. The latter declined from around one-half to one-fifth of all exemptions, while the former increased from one-quarter to nearly one-half. The relative contribution of each category of exemption refused by departments of state is shown in Fig. 3.1, for all years between 2005 and 2017.

Table 3.1 Privacy-related exemptions used by UK-monitored bodies in 2005 and 2017

Exemption	*% of exemptions used in 2005*	*% of exemptions used in 2017*
'Personal privacy'[a]	**24.9**	**47.1**
S40 personal information		
'Corporate privacy'[a]		
S35 formulation of government policy	18.2	6.9
S36 prejudice to effective conduct of public affairs	8.2	2.9
S41 information provided in confidence	11.5	4.9
S43 commercial interests	11.5	7.0
'Corporate privacy'	**49.4**	**21.7**

Sources: Freedom of Information Annual Report 2005 & FOI Statistics Bulletin 2017

[a]Shils (1966)

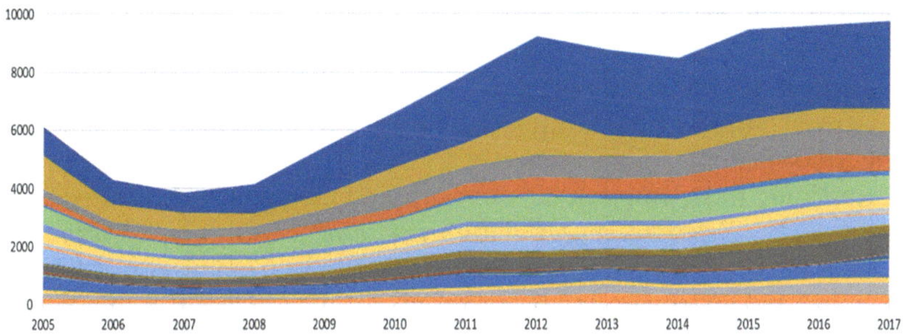

Fig. 3.1 Numbers of FOIA statutory exemptions used by government departments 2005–2017 (including 'personal information' in blue). (Source: Annual Reports of Freedom of Information statistics, Ministry of Justice, 2005–2017)

The relationship between FOIA and DPA was acknowledged as a potential source of tension in parliamentary debates during progress of the Freedom of Information Bill. Once enacted, in a leading case on the application of s40, Lord Hope commented that although the purpose of FOIA is the release of information:

> that proposition must not be applied too widely, without regard to the way the Act was designed to operate in conjunction with DPA 1998. It is obvious that not all government can be completely open, and special consideration also had to be given to the release of personal information relating to individuals. So while the entitlement to information is expressed initially in the broadest terms that are imaginable, it is qualified in respects that are equally significant and to which appropriate weight must also be given. The scope and nature of the various exemptions plays a key role within the Act's complex analytical framework. (*Common Services Agency v Scottish Information Commissioner*, House of Lords 2008, UKHL 47)

Within this framework, case law has established that matters of public interest may override rights to personal privacy. This development is illustrated in the following examples, beginning with one in which personal information did not figure prominently but was raised as a possible issue, perhaps a presage of future attention. On 4 January 2005, the education correspondent of the London *Evening Standard* submitted a request to the Department for Education and Skills for disclosure of 'copies of all minutes of senior management meetings at the Department for Education and Skills from June 2002 to June 2003 regarding the setting of school budgets in England'. Disclosure was refused by DfES, citing s35 and s36 exemptions, 'relating to the formulation of public policy and relating to ministerial communications', and where disclosure 'would prejudice the effective conduct of public affairs'. The *Evening Standard* complained to the Information Commissioner, who held that 'the public interest in maintaining the exemption did not outweigh the public interest in disclosure' (*The Department for Education and Skills and Information Commissioner & The Evening Standard 2007*). The Commissioner ordered all requested information to be disclosed, against which DfES appealed to the Information Rights Tribunal. Key features of DfES's case were summarised in the Tribunal judgment:

> Disclosure of the role and identity of the civil servant carried the further risk that accountability for decisions might be seen as passing from the minister, the elected representative, answerable to Parliament, to the unelected official. At the same time, it was unfair to the minister that he should be confronted by his opponents with his arguably unwise rejection of an official's advice. Such was the view of Lord Butler, among others. We were told that, whilst the Civil Service had been fully briefed on the implications of the FOIA, as perceived within Government, it awaited with some uncertainty the decisions of the Commissioner and the Tribunal as to how high the bar of disclosure under s.35(1) would be set. To uphold the Commissioner's decision on this appeal would set that bar considerably lower than was expected and would therefore be likely to produce the malign consequences of which we were vividly warned.

This view was rejected by the Tribunal. Dismissing the Department's appeal, the Tribunal observed that FOIA was intended to 'fundamentally' change the way that government was conducted, 'by replacing a Parliamentary Code with a statutory right to government information, imposing a degree of transparency, subject, of course, to exceptions, to which it had never previously been exposed and for which it sought to prepare'. The judgment includes an interesting comment on the application of s40:

> DfES raised the possible applicability of s. 40 (the Data Protection exemption) in the course of exchanges with the Commissioner … (but) neither in its original refusal nor in the letter following review did the DfES invoke that provision. Nevertheless, the Commissioner ruled in his Decision Notice that s. 40 was not engaged. The DfES protests that he had no jurisdiction, or at

> any rate should not have ventured to rule on a matter which the DfES was not raising … Here the DfES disowns any argument based on s.40 but is concerned, we understand, that the Tribunal should not offer any ruling on the issue, which may arise for consideration in a broadly similar appeal in the future. We shall certainly not do so, not least because we heard no argument on the point. (*The Department for Education and Skills and Information Commissioner & The Evening Standard 2007*)

As experience of responding to FOIA requests increased, so too did use of s40 exemptions. One in particular gained widespread notoriety, involving allowances claimed by members of parliament. Two main issues were involved: travel expenses and the Additional Cost Allowance (ACA). MPs whose constituencies are outside the London area are eligible for payments under the latter, as they require accommodation in two different areas. It was a complex and protracted episode, illustrated here with one request for details of Tony Blair's ACA payments, submitted by a journalist in the first week of the FOIA coming into effect. The request was rejected on the grounds that the information was the 'personal data' of the subject, a position maintained following internal review. The journalist appealed to the Information Commissioner, and there followed an eighteen-month period of communication between the Information Commissioner and the House of Commons. In a Decision Notice issued in June 2007, the Information Commissioner summarised the view of the House of Commons authority:

> It considered the information to be exempt under section 40(2) of the Act because it was personal data about the MP concerned. The House maintained that disclosure would breach the requirement of the first Data Protection Principle that personal data be processed fairly and lawfully … disclosure of this information in the detail sought would compromise the privacy of the MP and his or her family and that there can be personal security risks in disclosing where a MP lives. (*ICO Decision Notice FS50070469: para 6 & 10*)

In contrast, the Information Commissioner took the view: 'the link with holding public office is clear. If individual MPs had not been elected to carry out their role as public representatives they would not be entitled to claim the related expenses … It is only because such costs are considered to be expenses arising from the holding of public office that they are subject to reimbursement from the public purse' (para 32).

The Commissioner emphasised that 'particular regard should be had to whether the personal data requested relates to individuals acting in an official as opposed to a private capacity' (para 34), concluding that the information, with redactions, should be disclosed. Counsel for the House of Commons authority contended in an appeal to the Tribunal that once s40 was engaged, 'no regard can be had for FOIA' (para 44). Against this, counsel for the Information Commissioner argued: 'The existence of FOIA in itself modifies the expectations that individuals can reasonably maintain in relation to the disclosure of information by public authorities, especially where the information relates to the performance of public duties or the expenditure of public money' (*The Corporate Officer of the House of Commons v Information Commissioner and Norman Baker MP, EA/2006/0015 & 0016: para 43*).

Having heard the contending arguments, the Tribunal concluded there is:

> a balance between competing interests broadly comparable, but not identical, to the balance that applies under the public interest test for qualified exemptions under FOIA. (This) requires a consideration of the balance between: (i) the legitimate interests of those to whom the data would be disclosed which in this context a member of the public… and (ii) prejudice to the rights, freedoms and legitimate interests of the data subjects. However, because the processing must be "necessary" for the legitimate interests of members of the public to apply we find that only where (i) outweighs (ii) should the personal data be disclosed. (*EA/2006/0015 & 0016, para 90*)

An appeal by the House of Commons to the High Court was unsuccessful, and the information was eventually published, with leaking of additional details that would otherwise have been redacted. Media interest was enormous, as were the repercussions, with resignations by Ministers and the House of Commons Speaker, and criminal investigations into eight parliamentarians, four of whom were jailed. The case was exceptional, but established that within the requirements of the DPA, there can be circumstances where it is fair to disclose personal information under FOIA. The threshold is high, but an important element relates to the holding of public office. In another case, arising from the controversial award of a life peerage to Michael Ashcroft (because of his political and business interests, and tax status), the Decision Notice includes the comment: 'there is a greater public interest in placing the requested information into the public domain than, in respect of the specific circumstances of this case, to the public interest in protecting the interest which the honours and dignities exemption of the DPA is designed to protect. This is because there is a strong public interest flowing from the need for greater transparency in Lord Ashcroft's controversial ennoblement' (*ICO DN FS50197952 2010: para 69*).

As with the balancing of Article 8 and Article 10 rights considered earlier in relation to privacy and freedom of expression, the circumstances of a particular case frame the way in which FOIA and DPA are judged to interact. This has been reflected in many Tribunal judgments, and while these do not establish case law, a review of some examples can illustrate points at issue. The decision in the House of Commons case was used unsuccessfully by an appellant seeking disclosure of views expressed by members of a panel making recommendations on paediatric cardiology centres, with the determining issue being whether these individuals were 'public facing' (*Illingworth v The Information Commissioner and The NHS Commissioning Board, GIA/5435/2014*). The origins lay in the inquiry led by Sir Ian Kennedy into paediatric cardiac surgery at Bristol Royal Infirmary, which prompted a wider review of services across the country. Aiming to enhance surgical skills within a smaller number of specialist centres, a proposal was made in 2008 to reduce these from eleven to seven. Three specialist groups were to advise on the process, including an Independent Assessment Panel of eight clinical experts. Each expert produced scores, initially using the centres' self-assessments, modifying these scores following visits to each centre. After each visit, the panel met to agree a consensus score, and these consensus scores formed the panel's recommendations. At issue in the appeal to the Information Rights Tribunal was disclosure of the modified individual scores prior to reaching the consensus score. In response to a FOIA request, NHS London disclosed the individual scores, but withheld individual names. The names of panel members were themselves already in the public domain. The Information Commissioner supported this approach in a Decision Notice issued in 2013:

> The evidence before the Commissioner was that the individual Panel members were not, in this context, public facing figures but were independent experts in their particular fields. The Panel itself had a 'collective' identity and it was only public facing through its chairman. All of the formal scoring undertaken by the Kennedy Panel and which was ultimately used by the JCPCT was understood by those members to be by consensus of the Panel, and not as members individually. (*ICO DN 4 June 2013:* 32–33)

An appeal was submitted to the Tribunal, which summarised the grounds of appeal. Acknowledging the information was personal data, the appellant argued, 'the scores prepared by the Panel members were not inherently private and that the Panel members were performing a public role, so that a low level of protection was appropriate. He said that it was not reasonable for Panel members to expect that their identities would be kept secret. There was a significant public interest in disclosure, which was to allow the public to assure themselves that there was no risk of the scores being tainted by bias of individual Panel members'.

Dismissing the appeal, the Tribunal endorsed the ICO view that 'the Kennedy Panel members were not public facing. We accept that they were individual experts in their fields and were engaged in that capacity and as such not in a public facing role'. The expectation of panel members was also an important factor: 'it is, in our view, a cardinal requirement of the DPA that data subjects be told what is going to happen with their personal data and that any other use of that personal data will be unfair except in limited circumstances, not applicable here'. The Tribunal also commented 'that disclosure of the disputed information could and probably would put at least some of the Kennedy Panel members at risk of professional and personal embarrassment together with risk of harassment or personal abuse'. It explained, 'Unpleasant and inexcusable though this is, it seems to us that anybody becoming involved in a process which leads to an unpopular and highly emotive decision such as in this case must expect to be targeted in such a way. In no way is that statement intended to excuse such vile behaviour, instead it aims to illustrate that this kind of negativity is to be expected'.

The decision of the Tribunal was a majority one, with the dissenting member accepting:

> that panellists did not expect their individual scores to be disclosed but did not agree that the expectation was reasonable. He decided that the Panel members were public-facing and must have expected considerable scrutiny of their work ... He thought that the Appellant had a very strong legitimate interest in exploring whether the process had been fair and objective at all stages ... He did not accept that the threats to individual if they were identified was as significant as claimed, nor that release of the individual scores would damage the relationship between clinicians in the centres and Panel members. On balance he concluded that the importance of transparency in the process meant that disclosure was necessary. (*Illingworth v The Information Commissioner and the NHS Commissioning Board, GIA/5435/2014*)

Among many issues raised by this and other cases, two can be highlighted. The first is the extent to which officials are considered to be 'public facing', and the second concerns their expectation about disclosure and its reasonableness. The matter of reasonable expectations about disclosure was considered by a Tribunal in a request for information about the number of complaints against the Chief Constable of Lincolnshire Police that were referred to the Independent Police Complaints Commission, and the outcomes. The request was refused by the office of Lincolnshire Police and Crime Commissioner (LP&CC) in February 2016 as 'the information you have requested constitutes personal information', and therefore subject to an absolute exemption under FOIA. The requester complained to the ICO, who in a Decision Notice issued in August 2016 agreed the requested information was personal data, but judged disclosure would not breach the principle of the Data Protection Act (*IC DN FS50618842 25 August 2016*). The LP&CC was directed to disclose the information.

The LP&CC appealed to the Tribunal, which gave considerable weight to considering the expectations of the data subject. It concluded that in these circumstances a chief constable could not reasonably expect non-disclosure of information of this type. While the Tribunal accepted disclosure was likely to cause some distress, it considered this would be relatively minor. The Tribunal commented on the approach taken by the Information Commissioner, starting with the protection of personal information:

> Against those considerations, affecting the individual's rights and freedoms, the Information Commissioner set the legitimate public interest in disclosure – in this case the transparency of procedures designed to maintain integrity in the police service. She concluded the legitimate interests of the public were sufficient to outweigh any negative impact on the CC's right to maintain privacy in respect of information that concerned his public role. (*P&CC for Lincolnshire v Information Commissioner and Victoria Young, EA/2016/0217*)

A final example of circumstances deemed to justify disclosure of personal information comes from Melbourn Parish Council in Cambridgeshire (*Simmonett and The Information Commissioner 2017, EA/2017/0102*). At issue was the report of an investigation into the conduct of the Chairman of the Council, following complaints made against him. A member of the public submitted a FOIA request seeking disclosure of the report. The council indicated it intended to issue a redacted version, removing names of individuals. It then received a letter from solicitors acting on behalf of 'one or more former Parish councillors' indicating proceedings may be taken if any version of the report was disclosed. The council replied to the member of the public that it would not disclose information due to fear of litigation. This led to a complaint to the Information Commissioner, who upheld the decision not to disclose. The ICO noted that where information relates to an internal investigation, there is a strong expectation of privacy and, 'even among senior members of staff there would still be a high expectation of privacy between an employee and his employer in respect of disciplinary matters'. In addition, 'disclosure of the information would be likely to be prejudicial to the reputations of at least some individuals, either the instigator of the grievance or those who the grievance was against'. Acknowledging there was a legitimate public interest 'in allowing the public to know how an investigation into the actions of a member or members of the council has been investigated and the outcome of that investigation', the ICO nevertheless concluded that this was outweighed by the interests of the data subjects.

The appellant submitted a successful appeal to the Information Rights Tribunal. In a judgment in October 2017, the Tribunal rejected the ICO's approach, describing it as being 'of an over-generalised nature and shows a failure to grapple with the underlying issues' (para 16). The Tribunal substituted the Information Commissioner's decision with one requiring disclosure of the report with redactions of names other than those of councillors, the name of the complainant and of the Town Clerk. An important element in the Tribunal's reasoning is explained in this paragraph:

> The decision notice relies on an argument with respect to employees who are subject to disciplinary proceedings and who have an expectation that such matters will remain confidential. This is a misleading and inappropriate analogy. The report concerns the actions of a holder of a public office acting in his capacity as a public office holder. The reasonable expectations of that individual are therefore entirely different. Those reasonable expectations must be shaped by the Principles of Public Life (the Nolan Principles)

The Tribunal judgment listed the seven principles:

- Selflessness—acting solely in the public interest
- Integrity—not take decisions to further their own interests
- Objectivity—take decisions impartially, fairly and on merit

- Accountability—Holders of public office are accountable to the public for their decisions and actions and must submit themselves to the scrutiny necessary to ensure this
- Openness—Holders of public office should act and take decisions in an open and transparent manner. Information should not be withheld from the public unless there are clear and lawful reasons for so doing
- Honesty—Holders of public office should be truthful
- Leadership—Holders of public office should exhibit these principles in their own behaviour. They should actively promote and robustly support the principles and be willing to challenge poor behaviour wherever it occurs

The Tribunal concluded that public office holders could not automatically claim the privacy rights enjoyed by citizens in general. 'Expectations as to privacy of holders of public office are radically tempered by the clear obligations of office, for this reason alone the decision of the ICO is fundamentally flawed' (*Simmonett and The Information Commissioner 2017, EA/2017/0102*). Concepts of privacy are flexible. During the thirteen years in which FOIA has operated, refusal of disclosure on the grounds the information is personal data (s40) has become increasingly common, but although s40 as an absolute exemption is not subject to a public interest test, case law has established the basis for a balancing exercise which in practical terms is very similar. Having illustrated ways in which information disclosures have been obtained using FOIA requests, and its relationship with the DPA, Chap. 4 introduces questions around 'studying-up' of state institutions, to consider the contribution FOIA might make for exploring decision-making that is not otherwise readily accessible for study.

References

Ashworth, J. (2002). *Human Rights, Serious Crime and Criminal Procedure. The Hamlyn Lectures.* London: Sweet & Maxwell.

Cowburn, A. (2018, April 23). Majority of People Think UK Government Should Fine Facebook After Data Scandal, Poll Reveals. *The Independent.*

Digman, J. M. (1990). Personality Structure: Emergence of the Five-Factor Model. *Annual Review of Psychology, 41*, 417–440.

Etzioni, A. (2000). A Communitarian Perspective on Privacy. *Connecticut Law Review, 32*(3), 897–905.

Fuchs, C. (2011). Towards an Alternative Concept of Privacy. *Journal of Information, Communication and Ethics in Society, 9*(4), 220–237.
Gavison, R. (1980). Privacy and the Limits of Law. *The Yale Law Journal, 89*(3), 421–471.
Glancy, D. J. (1979). The Invention of the Right to Privacy. *Arizona Law Review, 21*(1), 1–37.
Halford (2015, July 30). Big Data and the Politics of Discipline. *Discover Society.* Available at: http://discoversociety.org/2015/07/30/big-data-and-the-politics-of-discipline/
Hern, A., & Pegg, D. (2018, July 11). Facebook Fined for Data Breaches in Cambridge Analytica Scandal. *The Guardian.*
Holmes, M. (2000). When Is the Personal Political? The President's Penis and Other Stories. *Sociology, 34*(2), 305–321.
Hughes, K. (2015). The Social Value of Privacy, the Value of Privacy to Society and Human Rights Discourse. In Roessler & Mokrosinska (Eds.).
Information Commissioner. (2018a, June 11). *Investigation into the Use of Data Analytics in Political Campaigns Investigation Update.*
Information Commissioner (2018b, July 11). *Democracy Disrupted? Personal Information and Political Influence.*
Information Commissioner of Canada. (1998). *Annual Report.*
Latour, B. (2007, April 6). Beware your imagination leaves digital traces. *Times Higher Education Supplement.*
Levenson, The Rt Hon Lord Justice. (2012). *An Inquiry into the Culture, Practices and Ethics of the Press.* London: The Stationery Office.
Lever, A. (2015). Privacy, democracy and Freedom of Expression. In Roessler & Mokrosinska (Eds.).
Lewis, W. (2019, May 2). MP's Expenses: A Very British Scandal. *New Statesman.*
Macpherson, C. B. (1962). *The Political Theory of Possessive Individualism: From Hobbes to Locke.* Oxford: Oxford University Press.
Manovich, L. (2011). The *Promises and the Challenges of Big Social Data.* http://manovich.net/content/04-projects/067-trending-the-promises-and-the-challenges-of-big-social-data/64-article-2011.pdf
Mill, J. S., & Lerner, M. (1965). *Essential Works of John Stuart Mill.* New York: Bantam Books.
Mokrosinska, D. (2015). How Much Privacy for Public Officials? In Roessler & Mokrosinska (Eds.).
Nagel, T. (1998). Concealment and Exposure. *Philosophy and Public Affairs, 27*(1), 3–30.
Rogers de Waal. (2017). Security Trumps Privacy in British Attitudes to Cyber-Surveillance. *YouGov.* https://yougov.co.uk/news/2017/06/12/Security-Trumps-Privacy/
Shils, E. A. (1956). Two Patterns of Publicity, Secrecy and Privacy. *Bulletin of the Atomic Scientists, 12*(6), 215–220.

Shils, E. (1966). Privacy: Its Constitution and Vicissitudes. *Law and Contemporary Problems, 31*, 281–306.

Thompson, J. B. (2005). The New Visibility. *Theory, Culture and Society, 22*(6), 31–51.

Turner, B. S. (1993). Outline of a Theory of Human Rights. *Sociology, 27*(3), 489–512.

Warren, S. D., & Brandeis, L. D. (1890). The Right to Privacy. *Harvard Law Review, 4*(5), 193–220.

Westin, A. F. (1967). *Privacy and Freedom*. London: The Bodley Head.

YouGov. (2018, July 23). Most Brits Think Police Suspects Are Entitled to Privacy Until They Are Found Guilty of a Crime. *YouGov*. https://yougov.co.uk/news/2018/07/23/most-brits-think-suspects-entitled-privacy/

Young, H. (1999, May 25). The Final Triumph of All the Butchers and Whisperers. *The Guardian*.

Younger, K. (Chairman) (1973). *Report of the Committee on Privacy*. Presented to Parliament, July 1972. London: HMSO.

CHAPTER 4

Secrecy and 'Studying-up'

Abstract Secrecy and deception are under-explored in sociology. Secrecy may be considered negatively in contrast to the more positive status of privacy, yet boundaries between them can be blurred. These issues provide a backdrop for a discussion on problems in studying the state, with attention to Laura Nader's call for 'studying-up' of powerful groups in society. Empirical study of elites is also underdeveloped, presenting many challenges, including access, and the complexities of multilayered organisations. A short review of opportunities and challenges in using documentary methods in social research is followed by a final section describing use of FOIA in research in the UK. Acknowledging ethical issues it raises, Sheaff argues it offers valuable opportunities for 'studying-up'.

Keywords Secrecy • The state • Elites • Documentary research methods • FOIA research

Secrecy, Truth and Deception

Secrecy and privacy have been described as 'intersecting but non-identical concepts' (Costas and Grey 2016: 4). Some distinctions can be straightforward, as when bodily processes that are not secrets are nevertheless performed in private. But in many circumstances, the boundary is less clear-cut. One significant aspect is a frequent normative perception of privacy as good and secrecy as bad, considered in these opening comments

M. Sheaff, *Secrecy, Privacy and Accountability*,
https://doi.org/10.1007/978-3-030-11686-6_4

on the place of secrecy in human interactions and relationships. For Simmel, secrecy was not to be regarded negatively so much as an indispensable element in reciprocal human relations. Simmel, examining secret societies, saw secrecy as a means of holding and sharing information in ways that promoted mutual confidence. 'We must not allow ourselves to be deceived by the manifold ethical negativeness of secrecy. Secrecy is a universal sociological form, which, as such, has, nothing to do with the moral valuations of its contents. On the one hand, secrecy may embrace the highest value … On the other hand, secrecy is not in immediate interdependence with evil, but evil with secrecy' (Simmel 1906: 463).

One direction taken by more recent work on secrecy examines it in the context of intimate relationships, including attention to cultural variation in these relationships. In European and North American contexts this can mean:

> access to knowledge goes beyond mutual offering of information to taken for granted privileged access to news, being trusted with back-stage and secret information … Because a particular form of intimacy is celebrated in European and North American cultures, featuring self-disclosure and expression of emotion, some analysts may resist calling forms of love relationships that are emotionally constrained and taciturn 'intimate', even when they involve a repertoire of other practices of intimacy. However, it is important not to be blinkered by a culturally and historically specific understanding of intimacy. (Jamieson 2011)

Although not the focus for this book, issues of self-disclosure, trust and sharing of back-stage information are fundamental for considering transparency and the private/public boundary. They also have relevance for examples of organisational secrecy that follow, particularly when this is viewed as a cover for wrongdoing or other negatively judged behaviour. Drawing upon empirical research into the Anglo-American Cold War intelligence operation, *Cobra Mist*, Luscombe argues secrecy and deception have not received the analytical attention from sociologists they deserve. Luscombe uses the term 'cover-storying' to describe, 'one mechanism used by state actors to inhibit publics from learning the true nature of their plans, intentions and activities' (Luscombe 2018: 402). Tackling a similar theme, Ball (2015) reviews public policy on terrorism in Britain in the period 2001–2008, focusing upon its setting within dominant discursive frames, including 'declining social capital', a 'battle of ideas' and threats from 'enemies of diversity'. However, a series of leaks, including ones following the 2005

London bombings, expressed alternative frameworks to which public policy had to respond. A notable example was consequences of the invasion of Iraq in 2003, which had been absent in official discourses. Exploring the role leaks can play in reshaping dominant public policy discourses, Ball argues:

> this case study shows that leaks of classified information reveal significant contradiction between the public and secret behaviour of ruling administrations. Civil society actors and rival political factions amplified these discrepancies within the mass media. The Blair administration neither ignored this criticism by using Goffmanian "passing" tactics nor confronted it directly by scapegoating leaders or those whose secret transgressions were exposed. Instead, the Blair administration articulated new frames that normalized their secret behaviour as an extension of their policy agenda. (Ball 2015: 116)

The framing of public policy discourses is an important route into understanding policy implementation, and as Ball concludes, 'secrecy is a powerful – yet understudied – tool for collective actors or groups who wish to shape shared understandings within a society because it facilitates the social construction of reality' (Ball 2015: 117–118). How then might opportunities for gaining alternative insights be achieved? The concept of entropy, developed in thermodynamics to refer to the degree of disorder in a system, is applied by Gibson to the control of information within an organisational unit. Suggesting that sometimes, 'social order is premised on a lie or a secret' (Gibson 2014: 283), he builds on the ideas of Simmel and Goffman through use of a case study, Bernard Madoff's massive *Ponzi* scheme. *Ponzi* schemes fraudulently use recent investments to pay profits to earlier investors. Seeking to explain how this survived so long, but then broke down, Gibson draws upon Goffman's idea of 'barriers to perception', proposing, 'six sorts of barriers that work to sustain knowledge boundaries and thwart information entropy' (Gibson 2014: 295). These are barriers to: knowing; asking; telling; perceiving; believing; and acting. Gibson concludes by arguing the public value of addressing these issues:

> secrets and lies are central to all manner of frauds, plots, cabals, cover-ups, black markets, man-made disasters, clandestine projects, and espionage operations. With the occasional exception, we as sociologists have not made a practice of studying these things, which means we have turned away from society's dark regions in order to discover whatever may be conveniently discovered under the light. That has left us ill-equipped to assist in the discovery of secrets that need to be exposed, and – though this is more controversial – in the protection of those that need to be safeguarded. (Gibson 2014: 303)

Another writer who drew upon the work of Goffman was Hochschild in *The Managed Heart*, her 1983 book that is organised in two sections, around private life and public life. Hochschild's work has its critics, but an important feature for the present discussion is her distinction between 'surface acting' and 'deep acting'. Surface acting involves presentation of feelings intended to conform to what is approved within defined social settings, irrespective of the emotions actually being felt. The smile of flight attendants in Hochschild's research might belie their genuine feelings, but they know what is expected of them. In deep acting, in contrast, the performance is not a fake but becomes 'real' (Hochschild 1983: 194). 'In surface acting we deceive others about what we really feel, but we do not deceive ourselves ... (in) deceiving oneself as much as deceiving others ... we make feigning easy by making it unnecessary' (Hochschild 1983: 33). Engagement in deceptive behaviour is not axiomatic evidence of dishonesty or insincerity. Actors may believe the predominant social construction of reality. Shared cognition and emotion can work in concert to form a blindness to counter-veiling evidence. When organisational failure occurs, subsequent secrecy should not be assumed to provide evidence of self-interest or corruption. The protection of dominant and mutually shared policy discourses is shaped beyond individuals, even when expressed through them. 'Studying-up' requires attention to issues of individual responsibility in decision-making, but this only makes sense within an analysis of the social setting. This can include political and managerial discourses, social networks and organisational structures and boundaries. Before moving on to consider a contribution FOIA-research might make, the following discusses the importance of studying state institutions given their position in relation to the exercising of elite power and challenges this faces through moves towards democratisation.

Studying the State

Despite the influence of neoliberal thinking on government-inspired transparency measures, as suggested earlier, a commitment to transparency commands far wider support. Four decades ago, speaking in May 1968, Labour Cabinet Minister Tony Benn gave what his biographer called 'the most dramatic speech of his political career' (Adams 2011). Benn argued:

> Nothing buttresses the established order so effectively as secrecy. The searchlight of publicity shone on the decision-making process of government would be the best thing that could possibly happen ... In this country, there is already considerable pressure to reveal exactly how the intricate structure of interdepartmental and Cabinet committees actually works. The more light we throw on the working of government, the less we shall have of the obsession with personalities. While the public and the press are denied the right to know what is being discussed and how decisions are being arrived at, we are bound to have columns and columns of personal tittle-tattle masquerading as serious political comment. (Benn 1988: 71)

Around the same time, Ralph Miliband was highlighting two features of the state requiring attention in his book, *The State in Capitalist Society*, originally published in 1969. The first, 'is the fact that "the state" is not a thing, that it does not, as such, exist. What "the state" stands for is a number of particular institutions which, together, constitute its reality, and which interact as parts of what we may call the state system' (Miliband 1973: 49). Secondly, he urged investigation of the administrative element of the state, suggesting this, 'now extends far beyond the traditional bureaucracy of the state, and which encompasses a large variety of bodies, often related to particular ministerial departments, or enjoying a greater or lesser degree of autonomy – public corporations, central banks, regulatory commissions, etc. ... the relation of its leading members to the government and to society is also crucial to the determination of the role of the state' (Miliband 1973: 47). Miliband's approach was rejected by Poulantzas, who criticised him for failing to appreciate the 'objective' character of the state, instead reducing class relationships to interpersonal relations (Poulantzas 1970: 70). This, argues Poulantzas, creates:

> a problematic of *social actors*, of individuals as the origin of *social action*: sociological research thus leads finally, not to the study of the objective co-ordinates that determine the distribution of agents into social classes and the contradictions between these classes, but to the search for *finalist* explanations founded on the *motivations of conduct* of the individual actors. (Poulantzas 1970: 70)

Miliband responds that the state involves far more complex relationships than Poulantzas allows: 'The political danger of structural super-determinism would seem to me to be obvious. For if the state élite is as totally imprisoned in objective structures as is suggested, it follows that there is *really* no difference between a state ruled, say, by bourgeois constitutionalists, whether conservative or social-democrat, and one ruled by, say, Fascists' (Miliband 1970: 58, emphasis in original).

For Poulantzas, the focus should be the *functional relationship* between processes of capital accumulation and state institutions, with the latter not considered an analytical focus of great importance. So, for example, he rejects what he describes as Miliband's 'false problem of managerialism' (Poulantzas 1970: 72), to which Miliband replies, 'this seems to me to underestimate the significance of the "managerial" phenomenon in the internal organisation of capitalist production' (Miliband 1970: 55). Soon, issues raised by Benn and Miliband were finding expression in Labour Party policy. The functional determinism of those such as Poulantzas gained little impact, as the state became an important site for democratisation. This included the commitment to freedom of information legislation in the 1974 general election manifesto. However, in noting this was not fulfilled, Leys later described the rise of an increasingly authoritarian state, undemocratic and bureaucratic. Arguing that, 'real democratization ultimately depends on ending official secrecy' (Leys 1984: 70), Leys acknowledged, 'the state is a complex terrain of struggle' (Leys 1984: 72), advising, 'democratization must be pursued with attention to the specific popular traditions and practices that will have to sustain it' (Leys 1984: 72). Expectation of widespread popular participation in decision-making is foreign to the British experience, he suggests, so alternative mechanisms for achieving checks and balances on authoritarian tendencies are needed. This point is developed further by Held and Keane (1984), focusing upon the relationship between the state and civil society.

By the 1990s the terrain of debate had shifted as the relationship between the state and the individual, rather than civil society, came to the fore. By 2000, Giddens was expressing the view that, 'state power can become stifling and bureaucratic', endorsing a comment by Offe that neoliberal critics of big government: 'must be granted the point that excessive statism often inculcates the dispositions of dependency, inactivity, rent-seeking, red tape, clientelism, authoritarianism, cynicism, fiscal irresponsibility, avoidance of accountability, lack of initiative, and hostility to innovation, if not outright corruption' (Offe 1998). Giddens continues:

> these considerations explain the emphasis the third way places upon personal responsibility, as well as upon the transparency and reform of state mechanisms ... in many countries the state, national and local, became too large and cumbersome. The inefficiency and wastefulness that state

> institutions frequently display provide fertile ground for the growth of neoliberalism and diminished the standing of the public sphere as a whole. As private companies downsized, adopted flatter hierarchies and sought to become more responsive to customer needs, the limitations of state bureaucratic institutions stood out in relief. (Giddens 2000: 56)

Giddens also makes a plea for democratisation:

> In what has become an open information society, the established democracies are *not democratic enough*. What is needed is a second wave of democratisation – or what I call the democratizing of democracy ... Old-boy networks, backstage deals, unashamed forms of patronage – even in the most established democracies, these were simply often 'the way things are done', accepted by those in political circles and by the citizenry alike. They aren't accepted as such any longer, at least by the wider population; and they have to be a principal target of the democratisation of democracy. It isn't by chance that new calls for transparency are being made, not just of political institutions, but in other areas too. (Giddens 2000: 61–62)

Some elites and 'old-boy' networks faced disruption. For example, the inquiry into high mortality rates during the 1980s in the Bristol Royal Infirmary paediatric cardiac unit found, 'the senior management was close to the "old guard" of clinicians and supported them. There was a "club culture," with insiders and outsiders' (Dyer 2001). In response, and in the face of substantial opposition from sections of the medical profession, New Labour pressed ahead with proposals to publish data on mortality outcomes in cardiac surgery units. But what Giddens called the 'democratizing of democracy' was not a prominent strand in New Labour, and some challenges to entrenched power appeared to create opportunities for the emergence of new elites. While the main focus of attention in traditional elite studies has been upon the most powerful and prominent groups, as in C. Wright Mills' account of the power elite in 1950s' America (Mills 1956/2000), the description of his colleague, Ralph Miliband, of a layered 'state elite' having greater complexity retains relevance for a research focus today. For Scott (2008), the concept of 'elite' applies to all those who exercise power: 'at its simplest, then, social power is a bipartite relation between two agents, one of whom is the "principal" or paramount agent, and the other the 'subaltern' or subordinate agent' (Scott 2008: 29). Elites operate, 'at various levels of a society and so are distinguishable by their degree of power' (Scott 2008: 36), with various organisational units of a state, 'generally unified through their inter-organizational links as branches of the higher-level organization of a state' (Scott 2008: 36).

Reference is made later to potential difficulties in adopting ethnographic methods in response to Nader's call for 'studying-up', but this may not be the sole factor discouraging attention. Savage and Williams explain what they term 'the demise of traditional elite studies' as a consequence of a 'pincer movement'. One part was, 'the rise of orthodox, positivist or neo-positivist social science', including a preference for large-scale quantitative surveys for researching social inequality. 'Given their small size and invisibility within national sample surveys, elites thereby slipped from view.' The other side of this pincer came from the anti-humanism of structuralist and post-structuralist social theory. 'The anti-humanism which was central to the structuralist movement of the 1960s led to a rejection of the focus on visible, human, elites, signalled most famously in Poulantzas' critique of Miliband's account of the capitalist state' (Savage and Williams 2008: 3).

Research contributions in this field remain limited, and often focused on economic measures of wealth and income. An example of an alternative examined connections between schooling and biographical entry into *Who's Who* over 120 years, finding, 'alumni of the nine Clarendon schools are 94 times more likely to reach the British elite than are those who attended any other school' (Reeves et al. 2017: 1139). Other definitions of the elite include Standing (2011), who describes it as, 'a tiny number of absurdly rich global citizens lording it over the universe, with their billions of dollars, listed in Forbes as among the great and the good, able to influence governments everywhere and to indulge in munificent philanthropic gestures' (Standing 2011: 7). Authors of another account, drawing upon Bourdieu in using indicators of economic, social and cultural capital, refer to, 'a relatively small, socially and spatially exclusive group at the apex of British society, whose economic wealth sets them apart from the great majority of the population' (Savage et al. 2013: 15). Here, a precise definition is unnecessary, as the meaning of 'elite' will be contextual, defined by the social relations within a particular organisational setting.

To illustrate, two empirical studies of changing state elites, in France and the UK, are briefly presented as examples. The first is an account of the emergence of 'programmatic elites' as a new kind of state elite within French healthcare policymaking since 1981, described as, 'a double shift in the sociology of elites' (Geneiys and Hassenteufel 2015: 28). Whereas conventional sociology of elites concentrates on the shaping of policy from outside the state, they consider, 'internal domains of state activity, each with a distinctive policy history'. This is related to the emergence of new sets of 'policy politicians' and 'issue specialists', possessing 'distinctive sociological and intellectual characteristics'. Geneiys and Hassenteufel suggest this presents a need for research to develop, 'qualitative data about the intellectual programs of elite groups in specific policy domains and how they evolve ... that uncovers complex connections between the constitutive elements of elites' (Geneiys and Hassenteufel 2015: 281). An important element in Geneiys and Hassenteufel's analysis is the ability of policy elites to mobilise resources: in addition to professional knowledge, this can include structural location in key positions. In this positioning, policy elites are contrasted with former 'technocratic elites', possessing three principal characteristics: 'they held institutional positions of authority within the state; they were specialized in a particular policy sector; and they were capable of acting as a coherent collectivity in elaborating and defending a policy programme' (Geneiys and Hassenteufel 2015: 291–292).

While Geneiys and Hassenteufeul direct attention to the structural position of elite groups in state administration, the second example highlights the role of discourse. du Gay (2008) locates his description of a new 'anti-elite' in the UK within the notion of 'market populism', which equates democracy with the market, emphasising diversity through choice and challenging traditional hierarchies. Public institutions were a key target, considered bureaucratic and unresponsive. Describing 'market populist' governments' approach to the civil service, du Gay writes: 'The long-standing Mandarin focus on deliberation and procedure, in protecting legality, consistency, fairness and other values, was not given a high priority by Ministers in successive Conservative administrations of the 1980's and 1990's. Rather, this ethos was contrasted negatively with the decisiveness and rapidity of action that was presumed to be the norm in the commercial world' (du Gay 2008: 94).

du Gay describes a continuation of many elements of this approach, following the fall of the Conservative government in 1997. 'The established doctrine that public administration should be conducted by a disinterested, non-partisan, permanent and unified civil service, embodying a professional ethic of office, and with a career path protected from overt political interference has been systematically undermined by the New Labour administration' (du Gay 2008: 95). The authority given to special advisers, and the proliferation of policy units, represented an attempt to turn the civil service into a 'delivery mechanism' for Ministers' objectives.

In du Gay's view, this attack on the elite 'Establishment'—led by those who refuse to acknowledge their own elite status—increases politicisation and opportunities for personal enhancement, while reducing political accountability.

Both these accounts address challenges to traditional hierarchies within the public sector, the emergence of new processes of policymaking, and new mechanisms for its implementation. A related feature of modern politics has been the development of a 'revolving door' between government and business, with retiring senior politicians and civil servants moving to positions in the corporate sector (Wilks-Heeg 2015). In 2010, the House of Commons Committee on Standards and Privileges investigated concerns about political lobbying, prompted by a television broadcast, which included undercover filming of members of parliament. The committee's report included an extract from one meeting between the former Secretary of State for Health, Patricia Hewitt, and lobbyists, during which she refers to an occasion when she intervened to encourage the NHS to consider use of the private sector:

> PH: 'I started talking to people. And basically what we did was work out who they really needed to be talking to, particularly at the strategic health authority level, essentially the regional ten intermediaries that sit between the department and the primary care trusts. And I was able to introduce them to some key people there.'
> 'Q: Are they civil servants at that level, presumably?'
> PH: 'They're NHS managers, they're not technical civil servants.'

Later in the interview, Hewitt responds to a question on meeting with officials:

> Q: 'How easy is it to kind of get meetings with civil servants and to be able to speak to them on behalf of your client?'
> PH: 'On the whole, I think it's never easy, um. But it depends a bit on the personal relationships and you need just to have a sort of eye to propriety and all of that so that, you don't put them in an embarrassing position. But I mean, I have regular lunches and coffees and you know, we're all mates really.' (House of Commons Committee on Standards and Privileges 2010)

In a lecture on the difficulties of studying the state, Abrams described the state as a 'social fact', adding, 'social facts should not be treated as things' (Abrams 1988: 75). Developing Miliband's approach, Abrams argues that the state is neither a physical nor an institutional object (such as marriage) but, 'a third-order object, an ideological project. It is first and foremost an exercise in legitimation ... the state is in every sense of the term a triumph of concealment' (Abrams 1988: 76–77). Presenting a challenge for research in this field, the final part of this chapter considers the potential for FOIA-research to explore this 'exercise of legitimation', introduced with remarks on use of documentary methods in social research.

Documentary Methods in Social Research

In her plea that researchers, 'should study powerful institutions and bureaucratic organisations' (Nader 1969/1972: 292), Nader considers four possible obstacles and objections. These are access, attitudes, ethics and methodology, which she discusses in the context of ethnography, and particularly the prominent use of participant-observation in anthropological research. Some of these problems are also considered in subsequent attempts to develop research in response to Nader's call. A discussion on the work of Gregory Button, whose work has explored the root causes of disasters, notes:

> Because he works primarily with technological hazards and disasters, in which issues of responsibility, culpability, and liability are central concerns, "studying up" is a central research strategy. However, in today's climate of increasing corporate power and (despite all rhetoric to the contrary) decreasing transparency, "studying up" has become extraordinarily challenging. Not only have barriers to information and access heightened but also, in our currently highly litigious society, journalists, anthropologists, and other researchers—as well as their informants and interviewees—run significant legal risks when they disclose the workings of powerful corporations or public institutions. (Oliver-Smith 2011: 648)

Similar experiences are recounted by Gusterson (1997), seeking to study features of the US nuclear weapons industry when she found a, 'laboratory shielded by armed guards and barbed wire fences. I was not allowed to enter, let alone do participant-observation, inside most parts of the laboratory' (Gusterson 1997: 115). Gusterson concludes, 'participant observation is a research technique that does not travel well up the social structure ... This technique may not be readily portable to elite contexts in the US where ethnographic access is by permission of people with careers at stake, where loitering strangers with notebooks are rarely welcome, and where potential informants are too busy to chat' (Gusterson 1997: 115–116). In its place, Gusterson adopted what she calls 'polymorphous engagement', involving an eclectic mix of methods, including informal socialising with scientists, but also interviews, and extensive reading of newspapers and official documents. With several notable exceptions, documents as data sources have been a more typical feature of historical rather than sociological research. In his classic lecture *What is History*, E.H. Carr suggested:

> The nineteenth-century fetishism of facts was completed and justified by a fetishism of documents. The documents were the Ark of the Covenant in the temple of facts. The reverent historian approached them with bowed head and spoke of them in awed tones. If you find it in the documents, it is so. But what, when we get down to it, do these documents – the decrees, the treaties, the rent-rolls, the blue books, the official correspondence, the private letters and diaries – tell us. No document can tell us more than what the author of the document thought – what he thought had happened, what he thought ought to happen or would happen, or perhaps only what he wanted others to think he thought, or even only what he himself thought he thought. None of this means anything until the historian has got to work on it and deciphered it. The facts, whether found in documents or not, have still to be processed by the historian before he can make any use of them: the use he makes of them is, if I may put it that way, the processing process. (Carr 1964: 16)

Use of documents in sociological research is generally traced back to Znaniecki and Thomas' *The Polish Peasant in Europe and America*, based on documents, including personal letters and newspaper cuttings, published in five volumes between 1918 and 1920. Subsequent document-based research developed in a variety of ways, and as Platt noted, 'it can hardly be regarded as constituting a method, since to say that one will use documents is to say nothing about *how* one will use them' (Platt 1981: 31). Plummer, for example, comments on the use to which Foucault put them: 'Foucault's use of documents is as a "text" where the human authorship is of no interest, where the subject is denied and where the informational value of the document is of little concern. It is merely an independent discourse through which power relations are constituted, and the text hence comes simply to exemplify this wider theory' (Plummer 1983: 132).

In a review of traditions in documentary analysis, Jupp and Norris (1993) suggested three broad theoretical paradigms in the development of methods, described with specific reference to criminology. The first is positivism, illustrated by content analysis. Just as positivist use of official statistics, 'assumes that the level of crime in society can be objectively measured and represented by crime statistics, content analysis assumes that there are attributes, attitudes and values relating to individuals, and that these are *represented* unambiguously in the manifest contents of documents' (Jupp and Norris 1993: 41, emphasis in original). However, as Prior points out, 'a focus on content to the exclusion of the manner in which a document is used could easily lead the social scientific researcher astray ... Documents as inert matter offer a very different field of study from documents as agents' (Prior 2003: 67). This provides the basis for Jupp and Norris' second paradigm, the interpretive tradition, which regards social phenomena as socially constructed. Meanings are assigned to documents, both by authors and audiences, and are not simply an objective representation of external reality. Thirdly, is the critical tradition, which Jupp and Norris suggest, 'brings a distinctiveness to analysis of documents and texts as data which differentiates it from the other approaches' (Jupp and Norris 1993: 46). Features include a concern with the role of official and other public documents, an emphasis upon conflict, power and control, an interest in the legitimising role of ideology, 'a commitment to not taking for granted what-is-said', and a commitment to changing the existing state of things.

What E.H. Carr described as the 'processing process' must take account of the purpose for which a document is created, not only its content. Scott (1990) suggests four criteria for the analysis of documentary records: authenticity, credibility, representativeness and meaning. It is difficult to determine these from a single document, but access to multiple sources can assist in assessing authenticity and representativeness. Credibility and meaning can be a greater challenge. Scott notes that credibility involves, 'the extent which an observer is sincere in the choice of a point of view and ... the attempt to record an accurate account from that chosen standpoint' (Scott 1990: 22), but comments, 'whether the author of the document actually believed what he or she recorded' is not a guarantee of accuracy (Scott 1990: 22–23). This draws the researcher in to an evaluation of meaning, which will almost certainly require additional sources.

Two decades ago, Ian Craib suggested the creation of documents was becoming increasingly important in organisations such as the NHS, so that: 'all interaction can be traced in written records which can be used as evidence in complaints that the rules have been broken, and can be used for reference purposes. This consistent recording of decisions and encounters seems to be on the increase, in the case of the UK at least, as a result of ways of attempting to make public services – the health service and education, for example – "accountable".' He adds, 'The way to establish that we are doing our jobs properly is to write down what we do' (Craib 1997: 140–141).

Recording for this purpose may not guarantee accuracy, or rather it presents a particular framing of the issue. An illustration of this process is provided in Garfinkel's analysis of clinical records, in which he contrasted what he described as 'actuarial records' with those providing a 'record of a therapeutic contract' (Garfinkel 1967: 199). The former can itemise each element in a transaction, equivalent to a form of book-keeping, while the latter can provide a record corresponding with normative expectations. 'Various items of the clinic folders are tokens – like pieces that will permit the assembly of an indefinitely large number of mosaics.' Elements are subsequently selected to 'make a case' for clinical activity (Garfinkel 1967: 202–203). Interpreting the construction of records in this manner, Garfinkel highlighted the fact that records, 'are integral features of the same social orders they describe' (Garfinkel 1967: 192). In a similar way, Cicourel (1964) explored the role played by official documents in constructing a person's 'delinquent' identity.

Being alert to the purpose for the creation of a document can be of particular importance, where organisational performance has failed in some way. These are circumstances identified by Prior (2003), as providing valuable research opportunities:

> In the normal course of events documentation has a relatively low profile in any organizational system. That is not to say that things, events and processes are not documented, only that such documentation is regarded as routine and thereby becomes invisible. At critical points, however, (usually when things go 'wrong', or when procedures are subject to an unusual degree of scrutiny or monitoring), documentation comes into its own. (Prior 2003: 60)

He goes on to, 'concentrate on what we might call organizational failure. Such failure is usually only traceable and accountable through the written record and therefore (from a research standpoint) crises in organizational life can provide considerable opportunities for investigation' (Prior 2003: 61). His research focus is on homicides in the UK committed by people who are said to have psychiatric problems. Prior explains, 'my main point of focus is on how the "organization" of care only comes into focus through documentation' (Prior 2003: 61). Writing before FOIA came into effect in the UK, his sources are Mental Health Inquiry Reports, published following a homicide involving someone who has had contact with psychiatric services. The advent of UK freedom of information legislation has brought a new method for research into organisational failure, an example of which is described in Chap. 5. Before this, the following section provides an overview of use of FOIA in the UK and the ethical issues it can raise.

Using FOIA in Research

The USA, with freedom of information legislation since 1966, has a longer history of the use of FOIA in social research, although this has not been extensive. A proponent has been Mike Keen (e.g. Keen 1992), who in one project used requests to obtain disclosure of information held by the FBI about sociologists (Keen 2004). Urging greater use of FOIA requests by social scientists, Keen suggests a reliance upon official publications limits access to valuable research data (Keen 2004: 5). More recently, considerable use of FOIA has been made by Canadian researchers, particularly in the field of criminology (e.g. Walby and Larsen 2011; Walby and Larsen 2012; Walby and Luscombe 2017).

In the UK, an early assessment of the potential for using FOIA in research suggested it, 'potentially extends the range of resources available to social scientists, and the experience of researchers in other countries suggests that it will be capable of providing a viable source of data for social research' (Lee 2005: 15). However, limitations noted by researchers who have used FOIA include an observation that, 'FoI is not a cure-all to the problems of access and disclosure with which researchers have always struggled, but it does give them an important lever when dealing with the traditionally secretive agencies of the public sector' (Brown 2009: 90). Referring to this comment, Savage and Hyde (2014) note suggestions, 'that researchers are yet to fully appreciate the value of FOIA to empirical research in the fields of social science and law' (2014, 303). For example, a review of FOIA requests in research involving the English NHS described the number of studies as 'relatively few', identifying sixteen conducted between 2005 and 2013 (Fowler et al. 2013: 6). Covering a wide range of issues, these studies involved a total of 1732 requests, with most seeking information across the NHS (Fowler et al. 2013: 4). Use of FOIA to obtain comparative information has been a common theme in the developing use of the method in the UK, illustrated here with three brief examples. Savage and Hyde (2014) used FOIA in research into whistleblowing, submitting requests to 48 food safety regulatory bodies, concluding, 'FOIA request are particularly useful where comparisons are sought to be drawn between various public authorities. By using a standardised FOIA request, data obtained from public authorities can be standardised' (Savage and Hyde 2014: 309).

Over a fifteen-month period, Johnson and Hampson (2015) submitted FOIA requests to 43 police forces in England seeking disclosure of information relating to criminal charges, the type of crime, and the nationality and age of alleged offenders. While noting limitations, the authors' conclusion was that, 'access afforded by the FOIA is valuable. Research conducted would not have been possible without this formal mechanism to obtain the required data; results received have been useful, interesting and informative' (Johnson and Hampson 2015: 263). In an example from social work research, Murray (2013) investigated free access to leisure centres for children in care through requests submitted to 152 local authority children's services in England. Results showed a differential provision, 'with fewer than half of councils (48 per cent) currently providing free leisure passes' (Murray 2013: 1347). Murray also comments on limitations in use of FOIA, including difficulties in asking extensive questions and probing responses, and potentially a reluctance by some authorities to comply (although she had not experienced this). She concludes, 'these limitations notwithstanding, there are many advantages associated with using Freedom of Information requests. It is suggested that it be considered a suitable way to elicit data across a range of social work topics' (Murray 2013: 362).

A common feature in these studies has been the collection of comparative data across public authorities rather than employing FOIA as a tool for exploring processes of decision-making. This context raises ethical implications, an issue considered by Nader (1969/1972) in her article on studying-up, and also by some commentators on the use of FOIA in research. As a method for collecting data, use of FOIA can increase response rates. For example, one study that achieved an 11% response rate, when inviting organisations to respond using a letter reported an 83% response rate, using FOIA requests (cited in Fowler et al. 2013). In the context of clinical research, some objections have been made that this undermines the principle of informed consent for participation in a research study, with complaints of, 'researchers using the Act to compel hospitals to provide data to further their research' (Breathnach et al. 2011).

'National and international guidance states that participation in research must be voluntary. This was written with research subjects in mind but should apply equally to work colleagues in the NHS. The General Medical Council, research ethics committees, and journal editors should consider the ethical and resource implications of compelling colleagues to participate in research, even if such compulsion is permitted in law.' (Breathnach et al. 2011: 1)

This objection deserves serious attention, although it is raised in a very different context to those considered here. One stimulus for the concern had been FOIA requests from a tobacco company seeking disclosure of research data on smoking and young people from the University of Stirling. Although resisted, an early report on this noted, 'a Scottish university may be forced to hand over detailed research into teenage smoking to a cigarette manufacturer after failing to block a request it made under freedom of information legislation' (Christie 2011). Most ethical codes on social research (rather than clinical research) acknowledge there can be circumstances where research is conducted in the absence of informed consent. On use of covert research methods, the British Sociological Association's Statement of Ethical Practice observes: 'There are serious ethical and legal issues in the use of covert research but the use of covert methods may be justified in certain circumstances … Researchers may also face problems when access to spheres of social life is closed to social scientists by powerful or secretive interests' (British Sociological Association 2017: para 14).

Use of FOIA requests, which may involve disclosure of information that the organisation would prefer not to reveal, can be considered analogous to covert research, and I consider there are circumstances in which this is a legitimate method to use, albeit in the absence of formally obtained informed consent. Ethical issues around anonymity present more complex dilemmas. The British Sociological Association statement of ethical practice, in acknowledging circumstances where covert methods may be acceptable, explains:

> However, covert methods violate the principles of informed consent and may invade the privacy of those being studied. Covert researchers might need to take into account the emerging legal frameworks surrounding the right to privacy. Participant or non-participant observation in non-public spaces or experimental manipulation of research participants without their

> knowledge should be resorted to only where it is impossible to use other methods to obtain essential data. In such studies it is important to safeguard the anonymity of research participants. (British Sociological Association 2017: para 15–16)

This last point is one emphasised in Savage and Hyde's discussion on the use of FOIA. Their starting point is that Freedom of Information requests fall outside, 'the traditional dichotomy between primary and secondary research'. By this, they mean that once disclosed, it becomes publicly available data, but this status is the consequence of the researcher's requests. Savage and Hyde reject the view that this makes it more akin to primary data, generated by the researcher, and consequently subject to the same ethical considerations as other primary research methods. They argue there is an important difference:

> In the FOIA scheme the responsibility for cleansing the data of personal information lies with the public authority to which the request is made. The data provided in response to a FOIA request should not contain information that identifies any person, living or dead. If this is not possible then the request should be refused by the public authority. Therefore, research conducted through FOIA requests will not pose ethical issues in the same way as research where data is gathered directly by the researcher. (Savage and Hyde 2014: 310)

This is true for the majority of social research making use of FOIA in the UK since 2005. However, there are additional factors to consider where the objective is 'studying-up', with a focus on decision-making by those in authority. In my own research, used as a case study in the following chapter, an important aim was to explore alternative accounts of an episode of organisational failure. As Becker observed, 'for a great variety of reasons, well-known to sociologists, institutions are refractory. They do not perform as society would like them to … officials develop ways both of denying the failure of the institution to perform as it should and explaining those failures which cannot be hidden' (Becker 1967: 128).

For reasons given previously, the protection of privacy through anonymity is important, but cannot be the only consideration. Public issues can generate questions of moral responsibility, for researchers as well as participants. In a different context, Phil Scraton, who led research for the Hillsborough Independent Panel, has questioned how far the protection of privacy should extend:

> Given the structural determining contexts of power, guarantees of confidentiality, privacy and revision cannot be offered to those who represent and protect the interests of corporate bodies or state institutions. A form of "public interest defence", more often attributed to investigative journalism, should apply to critical research into alleged abuses of power … the "public interest" ends justify means which, in ethical terms, violate the principles of securing informed consent from all participants. (Scraton 2004: 191)

Documents disclosed in response to my FOIA requests sometimes had individual names redacted, which on occasion I challenged, in some instances obtaining an un-redacted version. Within the legal framework, case law establishes level of seniority as a prominent criterion for determining justification for disclosure of names. In my research, identity was relevant for tracing relationships and networks, but even when these were put in the public domain through FOIA disclosure, with one exception, I excluded individual names in published work. The focus for the analysis is upon social practices. 'Public interest' is not an objectively given entity, but socially constructed, involving conflicts across the boundary between public and private. Rights to the protection of privacy and reputation are important but not absolute, and should not be a barrier to legitimate public scrutiny. For this reason, I did not apply anonymity to the organisations involved, which, 'would negate the study's objective of comparing public accounts with concealed knowledge. It would effectively maintain concealment' (Sheaff 2017: 526). To illustrate the value of FOIA disclosure in a piece of 'studying-up' research, Chap. 5 describes its use to explore a failed NHS contract, set in the context of policy discourse from which the project emerged.

References

Abrams, P. (1988, March). Notes on the Difficulty of Studying the State (1977). *Journal of Historical Sociology, 1*(1), 58–89.

Adams, J. (2011). *Tony Benn: A Biography.* New York: Biteback Publishing.

Ball, C. A. (2015). The Public Life of Secrets: Deception, Disclosure, and the Discursive Framing in the Policy Process. *Sociological Theory, 33*(2), 97–124.

Becker, H. (1967). Whose Side Are We On? *Social Problems, 14*(3), 234–247.

Benn, T. (1988). *Office Without Power: Diaries 1968–72.* London: Hutchinson.

Breathnach, A. S., Riley, P. A., & Planche, T. D. (2011). Use of Freedom of Information Act to Produce Research on the Cheap? *British Medical Journal, 343.* https://doi.org/10.1136/bmj.d6129. Published 27 September 2011.

British Sociological Association. (2017). *Statement of Ethical Practice for the British Sociological Association*. Durham, UK: British Sociological Association.

Brown, K. J. (2009, February). Freedom of Information as a Research Tool: Realising Its Potential. *The Howard Journal of Crime and Justice, 48*(1), 88–91.

Carr, E. H. (1964). *What Is History?* Harmondsworth: Penguin.

Christie, B. (2011, September 5). Tobacco Company Makes Freedom of Information Request for University's Research. *British Medical Journal, 343*, d5655.

Cicourel, A. (1964). *Method and Measurement in Sociology*. New York: Free Press.

Costas, J., & Grey, C. (2016). *Secrecy at Work: The Hidden Architecture of Organizational Life*. Stanford: Stanford University Press.

Craib, I. (1997). *Classical Social Theory: An Introduction to the Thought of Marx, Weber, Durkheim and Simmel*. Oxford: Oxford University Press.

du Gay, P. (2008). Keyser Suze Elites: Market Populism and the Politics of International Change. *Sociological Review Monograph Series, 56*(1), 80–102.

Dyer, C. (2001). Bristol Inquiry Condemns Hospital's "Club Culture". *British Medical Journal, 323*, 181.

Fowler, A. J., Agha, R. A., Camm, C. F., & Littlejohns, P. (2013). The UK Freedom of Information Act (2000) in Healthcare Research: A Systematic Review. *BMJ Open, 2013*, e002967. https://doi.org/10.1136/bmjopen-2013-002967.

Garfinkel, H. (1967/1984). *Studies in Ethnomethodology*. Cambridge: Polity Press.

Geneiys, W., & Hassenteufel, P. (2015). The Shaping of New State Elites: Healthcare Policymaking in France Since 1981. *Comparative Politics, 47*(3), 280–295.

Gibson, D. R. (2014). Enduring Illusions: The Social Organization of Secrecy and Deception. *Sociological Theory, 32*(4), 283–306.

Giddens, A. (2000). *The Third Way and Its Critics*. Cambridge: Polity Press.

Gusterson, H. (1997). Studying Up Revisited. *Political and Legal Anthropology Review, 20*(1), 114–119.

Held, D., & Keane, J. (1984). Socialism and the Limits of State Action. In Curran (Ed.).

Hochschild, A. R. (1983). *The Managed Heart: Commercialization of Human Feeling*. Berkeley: University of California Press.

House of Commons Committee on Standards and Privileges. (2010). *Ninth Report: Sir John Butterfill, Mr Stephen Byers, Ms Patricia Hewitt, Mr Geoff Hoon, Mr Richard Caborn and Mr Adam Ingram* (Vol. 2). London: House of Commons.

Jamieson, L. (2011). Intimacy as a Concept: Explaining Social Change in the Context of Globalisation or Another Form of Ethnocentricism? *Sociological Research Online, 16*(4).

Johnson, D., & Hampson, E. (2015). Utilising the UK Freedom of Information Act 2000 for Crime Record Data: Indications of the Strength of Records

Management in Day to Day Police Business. *Records Management Journal, 25*(3), 248–268.
Jupp, V., & Norris, C. (1993). Traditions in Documentary Analysis. In M. Hammersely (Ed.), *Social Research: Philosophy, Politics and Practice*. London: SAGE Publications.
Keen, M. F. (1992). The Freedom of Information Act and Sociological Research. *The American Sociologist, 23*(2), 43–51.
Keen, M. F. (2004). *Stalking Sociologists: J Edgar Hoover's FBI Surveillance of American Sociology*. New Brunswick: Transaction Publishers.
Lee, R. M. (2005). The UK Freedom of Information Act and Social Research. *International Journal of Social Research Methodology: Theory and Practice, 8*(1), 1–18.
Leys, C. (1984). The Rise of the Authoritarian State. In J. Curran (Ed.).
Luscombe, A. (2018). Deception Declassified: The Social Organisation of Cover Storying in a Secret Intelligence Operation. *Sociology, 52*(2), 400–415.
Miliband, R. (1970). The Capitalist State: Reply to Nicos Poulantzas. *New Left Review, 59*, 53–70.
Miliband, R. (1973). *The State in Capitalist Society: The Analysis of the Western System of Power*. London: Quartet Books.
Mills, C. W. (1956/2000). *The Power Elite* (New ed.). Oxford: Oxford University Press
Murray, C. (2013). Sport in Care: Using Freedom of Information Requests to Elicit Data about Looked After Children's Involvement in Physical Activity. *British Journal of Social Work, 43*, 1347–1363.
Nader, L. (1969/1972). Up the Anthropologist: Perspectives Gained from Studying Up. In D. Hymes (Ed.), *Reinventing Anthropology*. New York: Random House.
Offe, C. (1998). *The Present Historical Transformation and Some Basic Design Options for Social Institutions*. Cited in Giddens (2000: 56).
Oliver-Smith, A. (2011). Revealing Root Causes: The Disaster Anthropology of Gregory Button. *American Anthropologist, 113*(4), 646–648.
Platt, J. (1981). Evidence and Proof in Documentary Research: 1 Some Specific Problems of Documentary Research. *The Sociological Review, 29*(1), 31–52.
Plummer, K. (1983). *Documents of Life*. London: Allen and Unwin.
Poulantzas, N. (1970). The Problem of the Capitalist State. *New Left Review, 58*, 67–78.
Prior, L. (2003). *Using Documents in Social Research*. London: SAGE Publications.
Reeves, A., Friedman, S., Rahal, C., & Reeves, M. F. (2017). The Decline and Persistence of the Old Boy: Private Schools and Elite Recruitment 1897 to 2016. *American Sociological Review, 82*(6), 1139–1166.
Savage, A., & Hyde, R. (2014). Using Freedom of Information Requests to Facilitate Research. *International Journal of Social Research Methodology, 17*(3), 303–317. https://doi.org/10.1080/13645579.2012.742280.

Savage, M., & Williams, K. (2008). Elites: Remembered in Capitalism and Forgotten by Social Sciences. *Sociological Review Monograph Series, 56*(1), 1–24.

Savage, M., Devin, F., Cunningham, N., Taylor, M., Li, Y., Hjellbrekke, J., Le Roux, B., Friedman, S., & Miles, A. (2013). A New Model of Social Class?: Findings from the BBC's Great British Class Survey Experiment. *Sociology, 47*, 1–32.

Scott, J. (1990). *A Matter of Record: Documentary Sources in Social Research.* Cambridge: Polity Press.

Scott, J. (2008). Modes of Power and the Re-Conceptualization of Elites. *Sociological Review Monograph Series, 56*(1), 27–43.

Scraton, P. (2004). Speaking Truth to Power: Experiencing Critical Research. In M. Smyth & E. Wiliamson (Eds.), *Researchers and Their 'Subjects': Ethics, Power, Knowledge and Consent.* Bristol: The Policy Press.

Sheaff, M. (2017). Constructing Accounts of Organisational Failure: Policy, Power and Concealment. *Critical Social Policy, 37*(4), 520–539.

Simmel, G. (1906). The Sociology of Secrecy and of Secret Societies. *The American Journal of Sociology, 11*(4), 441–498.

Standing, G. (2011). *The Precariat: The New Dangerous Class.* London: Bloomsbury Academic.

Walby, K., & Larsen, M. (2011). Getting at the Live Archive: On Access to Information Research in Canada. *Canadian Journal of Law and Society, 26*(3), 623–634.

Walby, K., & Larsen, M. (2012). Access to Information and Freedom of Information Requests: Neglected Means of Data Production in the Social Sciences. *Qualitative Inquiry, 18*(1), 31–42.

Walby, K., & Luscombe, A. (2017). Criteria for Quality in Qualitative Research and Use of Freedom of Information Requests in Social Research. *Qualitative Research, 17*(5), 537–553.

Wilks-Heeg, S. (2015). Revolving Door Politics and Corruption. In D. Whyte (Ed.), *How Corrupt Is Britain?* London: Pluto Press.

CHAPTER 5

FOIA and 'Studying-up': A Case Study

Abstract The chapter begins by exploring the development of policy in the NHS in the early 2000s with an emphasis upon innovation and entrepreneurialism. This provides the setting for the case study, drawing on Sheaff's original research into failure of an NHS contract, incorporating documentary sources from official accounts and those obtained through FOIA requests. While the former largely attributed failure to exogenous factors, and errors by those in lower organisational levels, the latter allow a fuller analysis, for which Sheaff draws upon Diane Vaughan's work on mistakes and disasters. In light of these contrasts, a final discussion considers routes to concealment of information, including an innovative use by Sheaff of requests for his own 'personal information' to explore how his original concerns were investigated.

Keywords Studying-up • NHS governance • NHS contracting • Reputation • Autoethnography

Contracting-out of public services has been an element of UK government policy in the NHS for many years (e.g. Sheaff 1988). Associated with the emergence of 'New Public Management' (NPM), described as, 'a move towards a governance approach that places emphasis on transparency, performance management and accountability of public sector employees and managers' (den Heyer 2011: 419), 'NPM reforms can be

M. Sheaff, *Secrecy, Privacy and Accountability*,
https://doi.org/10.1007/978-3-030-11686-6_5

tracked to the ascendancy of neo-liberal ideas of the early 1980s' (Simonet 2011: 815). A fresh impetus to this drive came in the early years of the twenty-first century, and the framing of this policy in discourses of innovation and the entrepreneurial self provides the focus for the first part of this chapter. This develops to consider one example of a contracting arrangement established under this policy, using documentary material from published and unpublished sources. The latter primarily involved disclosures in response to FOIA requests. In total, twenty-three FOIA requests were submitted to nine public authorities, of which I requested nine internal reviews. Two continued to appeals to the Information Commissioner and the Information Rights Tribunal. I also submitted requests to five organisations for my 'personal data'. Attention is given to ways in which the subsequent failure of the project came to be framed in official accounts, and alternative perspectives offered through disclosed material. This example is used to consider the impact of 'structural secrecy', and the emergence of the 'routine nonconformity' and the 'normalization of deviance' (Vaughan 1999).

In addition to exploring processes surrounding contract, the study also investigated the handling of concerns by senior NHS officials. As this included responses to questions I had raised, FOIA requests were not possible as some of the material involved my own personal data, and therefore exempt from disclosure under s40. Instead, I made use of Subject Access Requests (SAR) under the Data Protection Act, through which quite considerable data was disclosed providing valuable insights into social practices surrounding the concealment of 'dark secrets' Goffman 1959/1990). Together, FOIA and SAR disclosures provide an opportunity in the final part of the chapter to address what Vaughan describes as 'clean-up work': 'Employees and organisations devote enormous resources to prevent incidents of routine nonconformity from being publicly defined as mistake. This, too, is worthy of research. The social organisation of clean-up work also has social costs that eventually are paid by the public' (Vaughan 1999: 287). My contribution in this chapter to this task is intended as an exploratory piece of research, with potential relevance for many other situations where the public and personal collide through the intersection of autobiographical or biographical narratives with organisational practices, such as is the case in 'whistleblowing'.

One final introductory remark concerns the citation of FOIA and SAR disclosures. Each can take the form of complete documents, redacted or unredacted, or of extracted information relevant to a specific request. An important difference is that information disclosed in response to an FOIA request, once released, is in the public domain. In contrast, personal information disclosed under the DPA belongs to the individual to whom it is disclosed. Wanting to encourage greater use of FOIA in social research, I have used a method of citation that allows any reader to request the same information from the public authority involved. Not only does this provide opportunity to test the validity of my own interpretations in this study, through challenge or replication, I hope it may stimulate similar use by others.

Where a complete document has been disclosed through FOIA, I have cited it as such, followed by the name of the organisation and year of the document's original creation, for example: (FOIA; Appointments Commission 2011). Full details of such documents are provided according to normal conventions in the list of references. Where extracted information, rather than a complete document, is disclosed, the source is similarly cited as FOIA, followed by the name of the disclosing public authority and date of disclosure, for example: (FOIA, Department of Health, 13.14.2012). As this does not refer to a particular document, there is no further detail to provide in the reference list. In either case, this enables others to contact the appropriate public authority requesting the same information. Two frequently used abbreviations are:

SWL&SG – South West London & St George's Mental Health Trust
SGNT – St George's NHS Trust

For subject access requests, I use a similar method of citation, for example: (SAR; email from Strategic Health Authority Chair, 24.11.11). Of course, others cannot request this, but it confirms the source and authenticity of the information being reported.

Framing of the Policy: Organisational Innovation and the Entrepreneurial Self

'What matters is what works' became a *leitmotif* of New Labour's period of government (e.g. Shaw 2004). While presented as a rejection of ideology, 'it is a feature of policies that their political nature is disguised by the objective, neutral, legal-rational idioms in which they are portrayed. In this guise, policies appear to be mere instruments for promoting efficiency and effectiveness' (Shore and Wright 1997: 8). Foucault's observations, 'on the way that language constructs the social world, the immanence of knowledge and power, and how the operation of power becomes hidden from view' (Jones and Exworthy 2015: 197), draws attention to the processes, even when they can remain concealed. The main objective in this chapter is to consider the potential for this to be researched using FOIA disclosures as a method. While the focus is upon a single NHS contract, much of its relevance lies in the policy genesis, and discourses within which this was framed. Specifically, information disclosures obtained during this research provide valuable empirical data for considering a suggestion from Exton that, although:

> government rhetoric portrays the NHS as prepared for and receptive to a new breed of entrepreneur to achieve the goals of its dynamic organisations … this ideology of entrepreneurship within the NHS may conceal elements of dysfunctional reforms, structured power and vested interests of the hierarchy both at national and organisational level. (Exton 2008: 219)

Former NHS Chief Executive, Sir Nigel Crisp, claimed in 2005, 'We know that entrepreneurial leaders think differently, outside the usual box as it were. This new breed of leader will be able to generate new and alternative solutions that extend the boundaries of healthcare … (entrepreneurial leaders must) challenge factors that are growth-limiting and refuse to accept the status quo – and that can mean, taking people out of their comfort zone' (Quoted in Exton 2008: 208). A White Paper published the following year described such leaders as key to 'unleashing public sector entrepreneurship' (Secretary of State for Health 2006: 173). Within a context of 'encouraging innovation' (2006: 9) and 'allowing different providers to compete for services' (2006: 10), the White Paper promoted external tendering of contracts for NHS provision. Specific reference is made to, 'supporting the development of the third sector and social enterprise' (2006: 175), including measures intended to lower the 'considerable barriers' to third-sector organisations providing NHS services:

> We will establish a Social Enterprise Unit within the Department of Health to co-ordinate our policy on social enterprise including third-sector providers and ensure that a network of support is put in place to encourage the wider use of social enterprise models in health and social care. The Department of Health will also establish a fund from April 2007 to provide advice to social entrepreneurs who want to develop new models to deliver

> health and social care services. This fund will also address the problems of start-up, as well as current barriers to entry around access to finance, risk and skills, to develop viable business models. (Secretary of State for Health 2006: 176)

These government initiatives provide the focus for this chapter. The DH Social Enterprise Unit (SEU) was established in June 2006, four months later announcing a 'social enterprise Pathfinder' programme to support innovative projects. Ivan Lewis MP, Parliamentary Under-Secretary at the Department of Health, later explained the selection process used to identify successful projects. 'Pathfinder applications were initially sifted at the Department against three broad criteria: (a) was it proposing a social enterprise business model? (b) did the proposal have commitment from a commissioner, or a viable commercial financial model? (c) was the proposal for a new service in health and social care or a new way of providing an existing service?' (Lewis, *Hansard* HC Deb, 8 February 2007, c1207W). Of 381 applications received by the closing date, 28 November 2006, 159 were removed in the first sift (Royal College of Nursing 2007). The remaining applications, 'were then passed to the strategic health authorities for regional assessment' against eleven specified criteria. These included, a clear sense of vision and purpose, a sense of innovation, robustness of governance arrangements and sufficiency of management capability, and finally, 'is there explicit commissioner support for the application, or a clear demonstration that the scheme will be financially viable?' (Lewis, *Hansard* HC Deb, 8 February 2007, c1207W). A further 177 applications were unsuccessful, following consultation with SHAs (Royal College of Nursing 2007).

Twenty-six successful bids were announced in January 2007, at a conference organised by the Social Enterprise Coalition (SEC). The *Health Service Journal* reported at the time:

> With the possible exception of the Houses of Parliament, there are few places you could expect to encounter four government ministers and a member of the shadow cabinet in the space of less than six hours. But such is the level of political interest in 'social enterprises' – businesses run with a social aim rather than simply a profit motive – that … all turned up at a conference in Manchester last month to talk about why the NHS and other public services need to better understand their transformational potential. (*Health Service Journal* 2007)

The report quoted the, 'former South West London SHA chief executive who is advising the SEC on NHS issues': 'Social enterprise is not just the latest passing fad. It's a huge and exciting global movement … The NHS needs to respond to this, and to allow people to own, control and participate in these new ways of working' (*Health Service Journal* 2007). One of the successful Pathfinder projects, Secure Healthcare Ltd. (SHL) won a contract to provide health care at HMP Wandsworth, but little more than two years later collapsed with substantial debts. A report in *The Guardian* newspaper noted: 'The Department of Health would not comment on the insolvency, but confirmed there would be no let-up in its commitment to social enterprise companies being part of the "plural and diverse" market delivering health and social services' (Gould 2009). Using published and FOIA-disclosed sources, the following sections explore features of the SHL contract more closely to highlight ways in which dominant policy discourses appear to shape decisions. This, it is argued, contributed to a 'normalization of deviance' (Vaughan 1999) in decision-making, whereby departures from organisational rules and protocols come to be normatively accepted, detection of which was made more difficult by 'structural secrecy' inhibiting information exchange across organisational boundaries (Vaughan 1999).

The origins of the contract award also lay in a highly critical inspection report of HMP Wandsworth in 2004 that raised serious concerns about healthcare provision (Her Majesty's Inspectorate of Prisons 2004). Despite the transfer of prison healthcare from the Home Office to the NHS, this was followed by a further negative assessment two years later: 'The commissioning of healthcare services by Wandsworth Primary Care Trust (PCT) was underdeveloped … Clinical governance arrangements were weak. The PCT had identified mental health and primary care services as priority areas for attention. Recruitment and retention of staff was a key problem' (Her Majesty's Inspectorate of Prisons 2006: 46–47).

A 2009 review by Wandsworth PCT explained the prison governor subsequently gave notice to the PCT of an intention to withdraw from the provision, and as, 'the local PCT provider arm was not in a position to incorporate these services, the Board considered that it would be appropriate to seek an external provider' (NHS Wandsworth 2009: 4). Coinciding with the launch of the DH 'social enterprise pathfinder programme', in July 2007, the magazine *Community Care* reported, 'a prison health care contract has been awarded to a social enterprise for the first time, it was announced yesterday. Secure Healthcare has taken over responsibility for all health services at the UK's largest prison, HMP Wandsworth in South London' (Taylor 2007). In line with government objectives, SHL were offering to provide an integrated service through coordinating services sub-contracted to two NHS Trusts. An audit report from 2010, disclosed in response to an FOIA request, notes that a context for Wandsworth PCT requesting this sub-contracting arrangement was, 'considerable enthusiasm from the Department of Health downwards, for a social enterprise model of care' (FOIA; NHS London Audit Consortium 2010: 8. Disclosed by SWL&SG). SHL received a £113,000 start-up grant from the Department of Health, and its formal launch in May 2007 was attended by the Parliamentary Under-Secretary for Health (FOIA; Secure Healthcare Ltd. 2009a. Disclosed by Department of Health). The organisation was chaired by the former SW London SHA chief executive (Gould 2009), also NHS adviser to the Social Enterprise Coalition (*Health Service Journal* 2007).

Structural Secrecy

Structural secrecy is described by Vaughan as:

> the way division of labour, hierarchy, and specialization segregate knowledge about tasks and goals. Structural secrecy implies that (a) information and knowledge will always be partial and incomplete, (b) the potential for things to go wrong increases when tasks or information cross internal boundaries, and (c) segregated knowledge minimizes the ability to detect and stave off activities that deviate from normative standards and expectations. (Vaughan 1999: 277)

Examples that follow illustrate the impact of segregated knowledge, a theme developed in the subsequent section on the normalization of deviance. Much of the evidence points to the contribution of cognitive frames in the construction of structural secrecy, themselves shaped by dominant discourses. The first example concerns evidence on SHL's cash-flow difficulties, one from a published account and other information from FOIA disclosures. In December 2009, a review of the failed contract by NHS Wandsworth reported that in response to requests from SHL, the PCT made advance payments from April 2008 onwards. Invoices for July and August 2008 were submitted in May and June, and on 21 July 2008 SHL informed the PCT, 'we do not have sufficient funds to cover our July payroll'

(NHS Wandsworth 2009: 14). An FOIA-disclosed audit review, commissioned by one of the Trusts to which SHL sub-contracted services, South West London & St George's NHS Trust (SWL&SG), reports on difficulties experienced in being paid by SHL, and notes that Wandsworth PCT's review described how it 'often paid in advance'. The audit report observes, 'There was therefore no reasonable justification for delays in payment by SHL … Wandsworth PCT has reported that they were repeatedly asked by SHL to pay early. This provided a strong indication of cash flow difficulties at SHL, but this information was not shared with the Trust' (FOIA; NHS London Audit Consortium 2010: 8. Disclosed by SWL&SG). Likewise, it appears the PCT was unaware of SHL's debts to the two NHS Trusts. FOIA disclosures revealed these were substantial. By the end of March 2008, nine months after commencing the contract, SHL had paid SWLSG £488,268 of £879,603 it was due, leaving £391,334 unpaid. Of £142,153.75 due to St George's NHS Trust, just £665.00 had been paid, leaving £141,488.75 unpaid. Together, the two debts amount to £532,822.75, and a year later, on 31 March 2009, this had increased to £556,222.00. By the time of SHL's collapse in September 2009, the debts amounted to £648,565.00 (FOIA, SWL&SG, 05.04.13; FOIA, SGNT, 30.04.13).

The contracting arrangement, establishing SHL as an intermediary between the PCT and the Trusts, driven by a policy aim of enhancing integration, served instead to increase the segregation of knowledge. Not only did structural secrecy apply within the local NHS organisations, other FOIA disclosures indicate it existed vertically between these and the Department of Health. On 4 February 2009, SHL was awarded a second DH grant, of £380,000 to develop a 'training campus' (FOIA; Department of Health, 06.12.13). This was the maximum allowed under European Union state aid rules. 'The Department's records show no indication that they were aware of, or had been made aware of, any significant financial risks associated with the organisation when it awarded the grant' (National Audit Office, personal correspondence, 12 December 2012). In addition, DH entered a Service Level Agreement with SHL: 'to oversee the supply and installation of digital X-ray machines in eight prisons in England for tuberculosis (TB) screening, and for the TB Find and Treat mobile outreach project … The funding for these projects was unaffected by Secure Healthcare's voluntary liquidation as they went ahead before the insolvency occurred' (Correspondence from Minister of State to Oliver Colvile MP, 10 April 2012).

Information obtained through FOIA requests indicates greater complexity. Initially, DH disclosed payments it had made to SHL of £25,200 in

2008 and £195,500 in 2009 (FOIA, Department of Health, data extracted from DH Business Management System, 14.05.13). These figures did not correspond with SHL's accounts, so a request for further information was pursued through an internal review. This resulted in disclosure of three further payments by DH: of £248,000 in August 2007, of £500,000 in April 2008, and of £1,457,682.50 on 4 September 2009. These amounted to £2,205,882.50, with the final payment made twelve days before SHL collapsed (FOIA; Department of Health response to Internal Review, 23.08.13).

The segregation of knowledge can arise not only through organisational boundaries but also from mental structures, shaped through dominant discourses, in this case, those of a neoliberal image of the entrepreneurial self. Morgan's metaphor of an organisation as a 'psychic prison', in which 'organizations and their members can become enmeshed in cognitive traps' (Morgan 1986: 202), offers a helpful route for considering examples of FOIA-disclosed information that throw light upon the processes through which departures from normative standards can develop.

Normalization of Deviance

Vaughan uses the term 'normalization of deviance' to describe a gradual process of adopting unacceptable practices which, in the absence of negative consequences, become the norm. Relatedly, Costas and Grey (2016) note how, 'organizational misconduct may be a matter of "organizational blindness" rather than intentionality' (Costas and Grey 2016: 49). Two factors contributing to such blindness are considered here. One concerns interpersonal relationships and trust, and the other the influence of dominant discourses. FOIA disclosures provide a window onto decision-making, where these two factors came together to create cognitive traps.

The first illustrative example starts with Wandsworth PCT's published review, which describes an, 'apparent lack of awareness of both Finance and Commissioning staff … that as far back as July 2008 SHL were stating that they could not cover their wages bill without having the following month's invoice paid in advance' (NHS Wandsworth 2009: 16). The review expresses concern at the PCT's, 'clearly stated contract payment arrangements having been altered without the approval of the Director of Finance' (NHS Wandsworth 2009: 16). No explanation for this is provided, but further insights into decision-making come from disclosed documents. Earlier reference was made to the health minister explaining the process used to assess social enterprise pathfinder applications, including regional assessment by SHAs 'against eleven specified criteria', and evidence of 'explicit commissioner support for the application' (Lewis, *Hansard* HC Deb, 8 February 2007, c1207W). However, FOIA requests generated no documentary evidence of this having taken place. FOIA requests submitted to Wandsworth PCT (by now part of NHS South West London) and London SHA seeking information on this process produced the following responses:

> NHS Wandsworth was not asked to provide any information or advice to the Department of Health and/or NHS London on any awards made to Secure Healthcare under the Social Enterprise Pathfinder programme in 2007 or 2009. The information is therefore not held. (FOIA; NHS South West London, 15.01.13)

> Following relevant searches, I have been informed that NHS London has not been able to locate any information relevant to your request and is therefore not in a position to disclose information to you in this instance. (FOIA; NHS London, 13.01.13)

Nor was this the only instance where FOIA disclosures prompt questions about adherence to formal process. In July 2008, SHL were awarded a £400,000 loan under the *Futurebuilders* scheme (set up to provide loan financing for third-sector organisations to assist them winning public service contracts), specifically in this case, to enable SHL, 'to bid for and deliver upcoming prison healthcare contracts'. Responding to an FOIA request for disclosure of information on risk assessment, the Cabinet Office stated:

> As part of the standard processes in place at the time, in assessing an application for investment a risk assessment of a number of areas including both the organisation's finances and the proposal finances was undertaken. As standard this included a review of previous accounts, financial systems, and cashflow forecasts. This risk assessment was presented to the External Investment Committee and was one of the factors taken into consideration when deciding whether to make an award. (FOIA; Cabinet Office, 19.11.12)

However, SHL's sole published financial accounts, to 31 March 2008, were not approved by its Board and auditors until 5 February 2009, so were not available when the loan was confirmed (FOIA; Secure Healthcare

2009a. Disclosed by Department of Health). Further FOIA disclosures revealed that when SHL collapsed in September 2009, £259,148 drawn down from this loan was written off (FOIA; Cabinet Office, 19.11.12). Nor could the approved accounts have been available for the Department of Health's determination of its £380,000 grant award, confirmed to SHL on 4 February 2009. On this grant, the National Audit Office (NAO) subsequently stated that, 'the Department [DH] held monthly progress updates with Secure Healthcare Ltd and received written confirmation from them that the grant had been spent for the correct purposes. However, there is no evidence on file as to whether this information was verified' (NAO, personal correspondence, 12 December 2012).

Correspondence between SHL and DH during this period was subsequently obtained through FOIA requests. These reveal something of the 'self-contained view of the world' (Morgan 1986), generating a shared enthusiasm that inhibit a more prudential approach. The following extracts are from correspondence during May and June 2009 between SHL and the DH Social Enterprise Unit:

SHL to DH (28 May 2009): 'I am writing to update you on progress at Secure Healthcare. Things are now going very well and we feel as if the hard work is paying off and the social enterprise is taking shape. We picked up a second contract to supply GP services to HMP Downview and HMP High Down in Surrey. We are through to the ITT (*Invitation to Tender*) stage for Norfolk prisons and Broadmoor high secure hospital and will apply for HMP Bedford. Swan House, our health and care training campus, is underway and I thank you again for the capital award to make this possible.'

'I am seeking a further £60,000 capital to deal with some unexpected cost pressures mainly ground works, equipment and security measures and I wondered if you might be able to consider that in year or a contribution? Our plans for 2009/10 are to win another 2-3 prisons, commence the training programme for health professionals and offenders, develop a strategic alliance with a GP cooperative in Devon to forward our work in the SW, promote our contact centre as a national resource, and build our community offender health team presence.'

DH to SHL (3 June 2009), copied to DH Director of System Management & New Enterprise: 'It's exciting to hear of the progress Secure Healthcare is making. The only funding stream we have available for pathfinders now is through the SEIF (*Social Enterprise Investment Fund*) which reopened under our new fund management arrangements this week – I would encourage you to look at our web pages with a view to applying. The application process is much faster now through we do still have to make sure that investments are state aid compliant! Were you planning to invite your local MP to launch Swan House. I'll try to call you later this week to chat it through with you.'

Note at end to DH Director: 'Secure Healthcare is one of the original social enterprise pathfinders, thought you would want to be aware of their progress'

SHL to DH (18 June 2009): 'Just a quick note to say we are thinking about a launch for our health and care training campus in August. Is that too early to get a Minister? Also great news, we have a good prison inspection and our contract has been extended for a further 3 years at HMPW. I hope you don't mind I put you as a reference for our consortium bid to support PCT's assisting social enterprises setting up under the "right to request"'.

DH to SHL (18 June 2009): 'Good to hear from you- fantastic news about your inspection! Please write to (Minister's name) inviting him to launch the training campus, please also mention that you are one of the social enterprise pathfinders as this may help! I'm not sure I will be able to act as referee for you – it's our procurement! Hope to see you next week'. (FOIA; Department of Health, documents disclosed on 06.12.13)

Given the severity of criticism in earlier prison inspection reports, it is noteworthy that the positive self-report of the latest inspection appeared sufficient to be forwarded to a very senior DH Director. When the 2009 inspection report was published, a ten-page section on health services included several causes for concern:

> Patients received thorough reception screening, but there were gaps in the provision of care, with only one life-long condition clinic being run and no immunisation clinics. There were a number of staff vacancies on the primary care team, resulting in an over-dependence on bank and agency staff and an inconsistency of approach to prisoners. Healthcare staff did not work as an integrated team. There were links with outside care providers, but too many external appointments were cancelled or missed. Dental services were good. There were a considerable number of pharmacy issues requiring attention. There were no inpatient services for prisoners with physical illnesses. Mental health services appeared good and were responsive to prisoners' needs. (Her Majesty's Inspectorate of Prisons 2009: 51)

The introduction to the report by the Chief Inspector includes scathing comments on senior management at Wandsworth and Pentonville exchanging 'difficult' prisoners during their respective inspections. This included two Wandsworth prisoners who missed important medical appointments as a result:

> Both were so distressed that they self-harmed. One, with a previous history of self-harm, tied a ligature round his neck, cut himself and was forcibly removed from his cell. He was taken to reception, bloody, handcuffed and dressed only in underwear. He attempted self-harm a further three times immediately after his move to Pentonville. The other took an overdose of prescription drugs and needed to go to hospital. On his return, he was nevertheless later taken by taxi to Pentonville. Those men, and two of the other transferees, were returned to Wandsworth immediately after the inspection was over. These actions were a dereliction of the prison's duty of care to prisoners. (Her Majesty's Inspectorate of Prisons 2009: 5)

There is no suggestion that prison health services were in any way complicit in the actions of senior prison managers, but the account offers a very different picture to the positive image shared with DH. This need not involve deliberate concealment or misrepresentation. 'False assumptions (and) taken-for-granted beliefs' (Morgan 1986) can encourage mutual optimism, reflective of and expressed through dominant policy discourses, serving to cloud a clearer analysis and assessment of risk. A further illustration of this comes from FIOA disclosures concerning discussions between SHL and SWL&SG when setting up the sub-contracting arrangement. The background lay in the Trust's appointment in 2006 of a new chief executive, who had previously been a Strategic Health Authority chief executive, before being a director at the Department of Health. A public report to the SWL&SG Board in June 2006 noted: 'The new Chief Executive will meet with the current SHA Chief Executive in her new interim role as Managing Director for South West London, within the London SHA' (Board report to SWL&SG, 29 June 2006). Following abolition of SHAs, the SW London SHA chief executive became Chair of SHL. The audit report commissioned by SWL&SG following SHL's collapse identifies concerns around the handling of risks associated with the sub-contracting arrangements, drawing particular attention to discussions between the two former SHA chief executives: 'The Trust included a 15–20% overhead in their bid price, to cover employment related overheads and any contingency. However, the Chair of SHL met the Trust's Chief Executive to request that this should be reduced to about 10%. This may have involved an element of financial risk, or subsidy by the Trust.'

Noting, 'there is no complete documentary record available of the processes followed during the period of the Trust's relationship with SHL', the report makes several recommendations on the need to conduct full risk assessments, report financial risk to the Board, and establish signed contracts (FOIA; NHS London Audit Consortium 2010: 6. Disclosed by SWL&SG).

Despite shared assumptions and 'cognitive traps', the contract arrangements did not go entirely unquestioned. The audit report states, 'documents provided to Audit show that some Trust managers informally expressed concerns about the suitability of SHL as a partner from an early stage.' This comment is mirrored in Wandsworth PCT's review, which states concerns about 'structure and governance arrangements' were raised at a PCT Board meeting, but explains:

> There is no further documentary evidence available that sets out exactly what these related to, other than a cryptic reference in one email: 'concerns about governance and financial flows which we will need to address in the next stage'. But none of those interviewed can directly recall exactly what may have been required. (NHS Wandsworth 2009: 11)

In terms of what Becker described as the 'hierarchy of credibility', these voices appear to have gained little attention. A consequence was that, as late as the summer of 2009, Wandsworth PCT renewed the contract with SHL, although again there are indications of concerns. The contract review was initially considered by a subgroup of the Prison Partnership Board: 'The subgroup found that progress had been made, other developments were in progress, but some serious challenges still remained. They concluded that neither termination nor a full extension was justified and they made a recommendation that the contract be extended for six months' (NHS Wandsworth 2009: 13). When this recommendation went to the full Partnership Board, the decision was instead made to extend the contract by three years, approved by the NHS Wandsworth Board on 29 July 2009 (NHS Wandsworth 2009: 13).

A change of chief executive at SWL&SG in February 2009 brought a more challenging approach. Extracts from a letter written by her to SHL a week after the PCT's decision to extend the contract are included in the FOIA-disclosed audit report:

> 'Since my arrival in February this year, I have had increasing concerns about the nature and operation of the sub-contracting arrangements we have with Secure Healthcare. I am writing to formally document my concerns which I

believe present a significant risk to this Trust. I have significant concerns about the governance arrangements ....

I understand that the contract between yourselves and NHS Wandsworth has been rolled over until 2013. If this is the case I am surprised and concerned that there has been no communication with myself or my team. In view of the risks that this contract presents us with as a statutory health provider, I would want significant assurance before I could recommend to my Board that this arrangement should continue.' (FOIA; NHS London Audit Consortium 2010: 3. Disclosed by SWL&SG)

When SHL went into voluntary liquidation less than six weeks later, SWL&SG was owed £525,064, which was not recovered (FOIA; SWL&SG, 05.04.13). As an example of an alternative voice to more powerful ones emphasising enterprise and innovation, the letter reflects something of a preceding tradition, with a, 'focus on deliberation and procedure, in protecting legality, consistency, fairness and other values', an ethos that, 'was contrasted negatively with the decisiveness and rapidity of action that was presumed to be the norm in the commercial world' (du Gay 2008: 94). Extracts from correspondence between the Department of Health and SHL presented earlier illustrate this ostensibly more resolute approach, but a review of disclosed documents covering the period from then until SHL's collapse reveal a considerable change in tone. Shared assumptions around entrepreneurial discourses, accompanied by high levels of trust within strong personal and social networks, had allowed a chimera to take a leading role in decision-making. On 9 September 2009, the SHL Board was advised by its chief executive of, 'serious liquidity issues ... A number of factors have contributed to the current crisis position. It is clear we have had poor financial information to track our progress and limited cost controls ... our cost control and management data has been poor from day one ...The grant and loan income injections masked the overspending ... The Wandsworth cost over-runs were not addressed'. Writing about the Swan House training campus, SHL's Board was informed: 'We went ahead with [this] development without a tested business plan' (FOIA; Secure Healthcare Ltd. 2009b. Disclosed by Department of Health on 06.12.13). By 15 September, email correspondence between DH and SHL include messages with the subject heading, 'urgent request for ministerial intervention' (FOIA; Documents disclosed by Department of Health, 06.12.13). SHL went into voluntary liquidation the next day, following which Wandsworth PCT took on responsibility for directly providing the prison services. Minutes of the committee overseeing this work highlight weaknesses in organisational systems, for example:

> It was far worse than first expected ... (Head of prison healthcare) was working on the structure as there had never really been one in place. (Wandsworth PCT 2009)

> This work was extensive and realistically it could take about a year to turn things around at the prison. (Wandsworth PCT 2010)

FOIA disclosures reveal that sufficient evidence existed from an early stage to trigger concerns, but those that were raised gained little attention. Structural secrecy and the normalization of deviance help explain this, but these were also a consequence of the cognitive framing by participants in the context of dominant policy discourses. The next section reports examples of official accounts of SHL's collapse, which did not have access to material described here, providing background for a concluding section offering an autobiographical account of using FOIA for 'studying-up'.

'Clean-up Work': Official Accounts

Here, I include examples of ways in which official accounts presented the contract failure. These generally attribute failure to exogenous factors, or identified any shortcomings as existing at lower organisational levels. An evaluation of the Social Enterprise Pathfinder programme had been announced on 24 March 2009, by Health Minister, Phil Hope MP, who told the House of Commons: 'The Department's approach is to let the Pathfinders make progress and then evaluate them. The Department has commissioned an external evaluation of the Social Enterprise Pathfinders.' The evaluation report, published in September 2009, acknowledges that, 'identified benefits were in many cases anticipated rather than being underpinned by robust evidence', and realisation of the programme's aims, 'is still at an early stage' (Tribal Newchurch 2009: 75–76), adding the surprising assertion that all organisations had low levels of debt, attributed to the availability of grants (Tribal Newchurch 2009). A news report of SHL's collapse, in November 2009, referred to the role of external factors:

> Insiders say Secure was sunk by a "perfect storm": being tied to a fixed-price contract that could not be renegotiated as crippling costs in NHS overtime and agency staff began to mount to cover long-term vacancies; a slow start to a new business that would have generated income; and the credit squeeze that made banks reluctant to agree a bail-out loan. (Gould 2009)

An investigation by the NHS Appointments Commission, in late 2011, expressed concern at failings by Wandsworth PCT, explaining: 'The award of the contract and its subsequent management and monitoring by Wandsworth PCT was distinguished by poor procedures and many failings in management. These have been attributed ... to the inexperience of the PCT's team in letting of healthcare services contracts' (Appointments Commission 2011: 7). In contrast, the review concluded that grant assessment processes used by DH were rigorous: 'The means by which [DH Pathfinder grant] applications were assessed and due diligence conducted from the outset ... was thorough, independent, open and externally reviewed' (Appointments Commission 2011: 6). The overall assessment was that:

> A review of the accounts of Secure Healthcare Limited for the first year of its operation show a solvent organisation with sufficient resources to meet its liabilities ... There are weaknesses and the Secure Healthcare bid team, I conclude, let down the company ... The underlying reasons for the failure of Secure Healthcare Ltd were typical reasons for business failure and they were addressed by the management of the company as they arose without success as it turns out. (Appointments Commission 2011: 11)

The review also refers to statutory duties of the liquidator: to enquire into the affairs of the organisation, and to consider the conduct of the organisation's directors. On the latter, 'action would normally be taken where there was, for example, evidence of negligence, knowingly trading whilst insolvent, fraud, etc.' (Appointments Commission 2011: 10). The liquidators are described as having, confirmed that they discharged their duties in both respects, and the absence of any subsequent action is described as, 'an important factor in the whole of this affair' (Appointments Commission 2011: 10). However, while the audit report to SWL&SG also noted the absence of any referral, a subsequent report to SWL&SG's Audit Committee provided further information:

> In paragraph 4 of the report, it states that the liquidator was required to consider conduct of the company's directors and make an appropriate submission to the Department for Business, Innovation and Skills and had discharged their duties. However, on seeking further clarification on that point, [name of liquidator] have now confirmed that there was an error in paragraph 4 and that as the company is an Industrial & Providence [*sic*] Society, it is not governed by the Companies Act 1985 but the Industrial &

> Providence [*sic*] Society Act 1965 and therefore the report normally issued to the DBIS was not required. (FOIA; South West London & St George's NHS Mental Health Trust 2011)

This anomaly was removed by Parliament in 2010, but the importance ascribed to the apparent non-referral in the Appointment Commission's investigation illustrates how clean-up work can operate through information inaccuracies, irrespective of the author's sincerity. I presented examples of contradictions between official accounts and FOIA disclosures to my MP, who raised questions with Ministers. Referring to NHS Wandsworth's, 'comprehensive review of the insolvency of Secure Healthcare Limited in 2009', the response of one minister notes the conclusion that, 'selection of SHL as the Prison Health Service provider did improve the quality of care provided ... Their selection, to the extent it was based on clinical judgments made, was justified' (Correspondence from Paul Burstow MP to Oliver Colvile MP, 10.04.2012). Another Minister explained, 'As Paul Burstow mentioned in his previous replies, the matters you have raised are about contractual arrangements between Secure Healthcare Ltd and NHS South West London. The decision to award the contract and financial monitoring are a matter for those organisation' (Correspondence from Norman Lamb MP to Oliver Colvile MP, 15.11.2012). The Minister subsequently added: 'I note that the view of the (Appointments) Commission was that Mr Sheaff's questions had all been dealt with, that a "thorough and carefully considered review" of all the issues raised had been carried out, and that it did not feel that any further action was necessary or appropriate on its part ... I am sorry that Mr Sheaff is unhappy with the answers he received, but there is little I can add to the information he has already been given' (Correspondence from Norman Lamb MP to Oliver Colvile MP, 08.02.2013).

Nearly three years later, I shared some of my findings with my MP, who raised questions about the scale and timing of DH funding with the Chair of the House of Commons Public Accounts Committee, who in turn asked the National Audit Office to investigate. When completed, the PAC Chair informed my MP that 'despite an extensive records trawl', only 'limited information' was available. For one payment, 'the Department could not find a business case ... and so the exact nature of what this payment was for could not be ascertained'. Explaining the policy for records retention, she adds, 'unfortunately, some records of enduring value were not identified as such at the time and are no longer available'. At the end of the letter, the PAC Chair adds a handwritten note, 'I will raise questions about record keeping as a result of your enquiry' (Correspondence from Meg Hillier MP to Oliver Colvile MP, 08.01.2016).

Studying-up: A Sociological Autobiography

The chapter concludes with an autobiographical account of the process, through which the failed NHS contract became a subject for research. In the summer of 2013, piecing together information, I developed a preliminary research design based around use of FOIA. Several years before, I had read and been captivated by Diane Vaughan's meticulous sociological account of the *Challenger* spaceship disaster, and I reflected again on her reference to the role of 'clean-up work'. Notes I wrote in June 2013 explained:

> Eighteen months after first raising questions, I had been able to establish through formal NHS processes little more than that many core concerns had not been investigated. I was advised it would not be possible to pursue this as the organisations were being abolished as a result of the Health and Social Care Act … I now understand that it is the "clean up work" that concerns me more than the original issue itself.

I became aware of the SHL contract through my role as a Non-Executive Director of Plymouth Primary Care Trust (PCT), encountering from the outset an extraordinary reluctance from those in authority to respond to questions. My writing now constitutes a form of retrospective participant-observation which, 'might be described as "experience recollected in academia". A number of distinguished observational studies have been conducted (at least partially) retrospectively, after the event'. (Bulmer 1982: 232). Friedman develops this point:

> Expressed more broadly, retrospective participant observation constitutes an autobiographical sociology, whereby the sociologist probes one or more past personal experiences as a way of identifying and analysing something sociologically relevant. Autobiographical sociology, as a pathway to data and ideas, requires that the sociologist introspectively recollect, reconstruct and interpret the past phenomenon or process he/she was involved in. (Friedman 1990: 61)

This brings risks, not least because, 'literal description is simply not possible. Even the most careful of ethnographic descriptions, for example, are actually rigorous combinations of selectivity and interpretation' (Stanley 1993: 49). As Plummer comments, '"acts of writing" help us see that lives are always "composed" and that it may be the very act of composition itself which lies at the heart of the auto/biographical mode. It is not the real life but the composed life' (Plummer 2001: 88). Consequently, my own account bears the imprint of selectivity no less than appeared in official accounts, but in offering a description of how and why I moved from the role of participant to that of researcher, I hope to contribute further insights into the performance of 'clean-up work'. Data on which this account is based are largely drawn from documents disclosed in response to my subject access requests for 'personal information'.

To set this in context, in July 2010, the Secretary of State for Health, Andrew Lansley, issued a White Paper, *Equity and excellence: Liberating the NHS*, which, among other changes, proposed the abolition of PCTs, to be replaced by Clinical Commissioning Groups. Changes came into effect in 2013, following passage of the Health and Social Care Act 2012, but as early as December 2010, the Department of Health published an 'operating framework', described by the Chief Executive of the NHS, Sir David Nicholson, as, 'beginning in earnest the transition to the new system'. PCTs were required to join together into 'clusters', to be overseen by SHAs. By early April 2011, opposition caused the government to announce it would, 'pause, listen, reflect and improve' its plans for the NHS. On the ground, things felt very different as the rapid pace of change continued. I raised concerns about transparency and accountability, including questions in one email about the contract involving SHL (by this time its former Chair was a NHS Non-Executive Director). My email was forwarded to the SHA Chair, Mr Charles Howeson, and the SHA chief executive, and the regional commissioner for the Appointments Commission (the body responsible for appointing NHS Non-Executive Directors). My PCT Chair received a letter from the SHA Chair, which included the comment, 'I have not been impressed by the disruption caused by one of your Non-Executives'. Another letter written by the SHA Chair, to the Appointments Commission, later became the focus for an FOIA request, including an appeal to the Information Tribunal. Several extracts were disclosed, but the Tribunal concluded the letter contained personal data of individuals, including, 'Mr Howeson himself whose opinions are his personal data. He is identified as author in the disclosed redacted version of the letter and no further consideration of his rights is necessary since such personal data are the personal data of one or more of the other data subjects in any event' (*Sheaff and The Information Commissioner & The Department of Health, EA/2014/0005: para 19*). In a written statement submitted to the Tribunal hearing, Mr Howeson explained: 'I wish to make it clear that I am firmly of the view that it would not be in the public interest for the Department of Health to release any further information or indeed to indulge in further correspondence with MS' (*Statement submitted to Information Rights Tribunal, Sheaff and The Information Commissioner & The Department of Health, EA/2014/0005*). The identification of an opinion as the personal data of its holder is returned to later, but it was evident at the time that the SHA sought to discourage questions. My PCT Chair later explained, 'Mr Howeson was very critical of me at the time. In his view I should have stopped my board colleague from pursuing the matter. He knew I disagreed' (Written statement submitted to Information Rights Tribunal, *Sheaff and The Information Commissioner & The Department of Health, EA/2014/0005*).

I wrote to the SHA Chair detailing my concerns. I explained, 'As this issue arose from questions I asked of xxxxx there is unfortunately but inevitably a focus upon the individual in what follows. However, the broader issues raised are the ones that really concern me: governance, risk management, and public confidence, in particular.' I added: 'I am absolutely convinced that the motives behind the endeavour reflected a genuine ambition to bring much needed improvements in prison healthcare at HMP Wandsworth.' However, I sought to justify my criticism of his behaviour: 'This is public money, and I am alarmed that you appear to be using your position as Chairman of the SHA to object to questions about this being raised' (FOIA; Letter from Mike Sheaff to Charles Howeson, South West Strategic Health Authority Chair. Disclosed by Department of Health, 06.12.13). Having copied this letter to local MPs, I soon learned that my PCT Chair was required to engage in a telephone conference call with the SHA Chair, a transcript of which I subsequently obtained through a subject access request. Early in the conversation the SHA Chair refers to, 'Mike Sheaff's letter to all and sundry', to which the PCT Chair comments, 'he sent it only to those people he thought ... it is not in the public domain is it?' Later on, the SHA Chair expresses 'surprise and disappointment' that, 'he has passed (information) outside the National Health Service and you say if you pass it to Members of Parliament it is not in the public domain. I beg to differ. Members of Parliament *are* the public domain' (emphasis in original transcript). Expressing his concern that a NHS Chair should, 'allow a Non-Executive Director to write about NHS matters to Members of Parliament', the SHA Chair explained, 'I am not comfortable with running *my* bit of the NHS with all the information that is privy to subordinate Boards being dished out to Members of Parliament without the sanction of the Chair' (SAR; South West Strategic Health Authority Chair in telephone conference call, 15.09.11. Emphasis in original transcript).

I was told the Appointments Commission would investigate my concerns, and following its completion the SHA Chair wrote to local MPs to inform them:

> 'A very detailed and thorough formal investigation triggered by Mike Sheaff's communications was undertaken by the Chair of Audit of the NHS Appointments Commission. It took two months to complete and involved review of over 450 pages of documents from 45 personal and organisational reference sources….
>
> I trust all touched by this regrettable episode will take the opportunity to reflect carefully upon the definitive findings of this rigorous investigation and the unwarranted embarrassment and distress caused to a dedicated and very able NHS Chair by the manner in which concerns that were subsequently found to be completely unfounded and in the words of the senior investigating officer, "wholly inappropriately shared."' (SAR; Letter from SHA Chair to MP's and others, December 2011)

Much later, after subject access requests, FOIA disclosures and further reflection, I formed a view that clean-up work can involve a pattern of separate but related elements. It remains an under-researched area, and with the aim of stimulating discussion, I illustrate how I categorised these in terms of framing, funnelling and repudiation. These were not strictly chronological stages, as they overlap and interact, but for ease of description, examples are provided using this sequence of headings.

Framing

Two features came to the fore when examining how my original concerns raised as a Non-Executive Director were framed. First, they were presented exclusively as a criticism of an individual, and secondly, the sharing of information with MPs was deemed 'wholly inappropriate'. Ascribing to me the status of an 'outsider', recalled Goffman's observation on a team member who, 'sells out the show to the audience ... If it appears that the individual first joined the team in a sincere way and not with the premeditated plan of disclosing its secrets, we sometimes call him a traitor, turncoat or quitter' (Goffman 1959: 145).

An example of how documentary records can provide differing versions of events arose from a telephone call between the SHA Chair and a member of my own PCT administrative team. The call concerned attempts to arrange a meeting between myself, the SHA Chair and my PCT Chair. A record of the conversation written by the SHA Chair was obtained through a subject access request, in which he explains:

> I have just been telephoned back by (member of administrative team) who I sensed was squirming with embarrassment, to be told ... she could get no decision out of either of them and that both were out of contact ... the Strategic Health Authority and the Appointments Commission are now being treated with an unacceptable degree of contempt ... (member of the administrative team) has thus been deliberately manoeuvred into taking a direct degree of blame for this, quite unfairly ... this behaviour towards a member of staff, which is clearly damaging to them is absolutely reprehensible in itself and totally unacceptable in the NHS. (SAR; email from SHA Chair to several recipients with subject heading 'Urgent – Plymouth', 24.11.11)

A contrasting account of the same conversation, provided shortly after the episode by the member of the administrative team involved to the person's line manager, was shared with me. After informing the SHA Chair that the PCT Chair and I were not available, the account reports, 'he proceeded to shout at me that, "this was unacceptable, and as the Chair of the SHA, if he requests a meeting, they should accommodate his wishes"'. The explanation offered, 'did not make any difference to (the SHA Chair) who continued to shout at me that he was the Chair and that they should be more flexible to meet with him and that their behaviour was unacceptable. He then continued to rant for a couple more minutes' (Personal correspondence with author of the letter, dated 03.12.11).

Another illustration of the relationship between documentary records and hierarchies of credibility (Becker 1967) came in a letter I received form the SHA Chair following completion of the Appointments Commission investigation. He explained he would, 'be writing in confidence to all whom I know to have been brought into this matter. I shall additionally write to the Appointments Commission to thank them for their prompt and thorough investigation and to ask that their findings, together with copies of my correspondences, be held on file for consideration by the Commission and its successor body as needs determine' The letter concluded, 'Subsequent to the above this matter is, from the perspective of NHS South of England deemed to have been appropriately investigated and formally closed and no further communication shall be entered into' (Personal correspondence from SHA Chair to Mike Sheaff, 01.12.11). Documents disclosed in response to SARs included confirmation that my request to see the Appointments Commission report would be rejected 'for reputational reasons' (SAR; 'A briefing by the SHA on the Mike Sheaff issue as at 20 December 2011', NHS South of England).

I nevertheless secured a meeting, in January 2012, with the Appointment Commission's Human Resources Advisor. The AC chief executive subsequently explained to me, 'different parties have interpreted events and communications somewhat differently ... and it is unlikely further exchanges will diminish these differences' (Personal correspondence from Appointments Commission chief executive, 27.01.12). I learned later more about the framing of my concerns from a redacted copy of the HR advisor's report. The purpose of the meeting is described as, 'Mike Sheaff be called to explain why he felt obliged and entitled to investigate and why having done so failed to follow appropriate procedures'. The last point referred to my contact with MPs, about which the HR adviser complained:

> This was an invidious position for the NHS to have been placed in and entirely a consequence of Mike Sheaff's failure to follow proper procedures ... The reasons given by Mike Sheaff for mounting his own investigation are tenuous at best ... Neither the NHS South of England or Commission could have reasonably anticipated the decision by Mike Sheaff to share his concerns within and outside the NHS. His reasons for doing so are unconvincing and contradictory. (SAR; 'Report into concerns raised by Mike Sheaff', 27.01.12. Disclosed by Appointments Commission)

Funnelling

Working in concert with framing, funnelling describes ways in which jurisdictional boundaries served to fragment and dilute accountabilities. An early example came in the letter from the AC chief executive, referring to the advice of their HR adviser who, 'notes your own continuing concerns in respect of allocation of public funds to business ventures but as he rightly observes this does not fall within the purview of the Commission' (Personal correspondence from Appointments Commission chief executive, 27.01.12). Funnelling of this type creates significant obstacles to effective scrutiny. One example was when, having obtained a copy of the AC report, I felt important issues concerning governance were not addressed. Seeking an explanation from the AC, I was told:

> It would not have been appropriate for the Appointments Commission, with its very clearly defined role in relation to the appointment of chairs and non-executive directors of NHS bodies, to consider the efficacy or otherwise of the decision making processes in the wider NHS, even in so far as they have implications for good governance. The terms of reference for (the) review was similarly clearly defined and restricted to consider those matters that were appropriate for the Appointments Commission to consider. (Correspondence from Appointments Commission Acting Chief Executive, 26.09.2012)

However, a similar question I pursued with the SHA prompted a very different response:

> You have questioned why the issues you raised that went beyond the remit of the NHS Appointments Commission were not investigated. You have referred to "the broader issues raised are the ones that concern me: governance, risk management and public confidence in particular" … All the matters you raised in your original email and subsequent letter were investigated and decided upon … those broader issues were addressed and I do not see there are any outstanding matters to take forward. (Personal correspondence from South of England SHA Chair, 30.05.12)

Early in the whole process, the SHA appointed a lawyer to act on its behalf, who continued to present his client's case that my concerns had all been addressed by the Appointments Commission. Examples include:

> My Client is satisfied that the concerns you raised have been fully investigated and that they are unfounded. (Personal correspondence from SHA lawyer, 02.10.12)

> You have previously raised the concerns you had regarding NHS governance and decision-making. These have been thoroughly looked at and my Client has dealt with all the issues you raised in that regard. (Personal correspondence from SHA lawyer, 14.11.12)

> You make reference ... to the concerns you raised regarding Secure Healthcare. As I stated in my email of 2 October, my Client is satisfied that such concerns have been fully investigated and that they are unfounded. (Personal correspondence from SHA lawyer, 19.12.12)

In the absence of a meaningful response, I complained to the Parliamentary and Health Service Ombudsman (PHSO) about the SHA's handling of my complaint, but was informed:

> Although you said you want us to look at the SHA's complaint handling only, the substance of your complaint appears to relate to how the issues you raised about the recently appointed Chair of the Cluster were handled and the subsequent allegation that you have been disruptive in raising these ... We are unable to consider such matters and the handling of a complaint about these issues is also excluded from our consideration. (Personal correspondence from PHSO, 21.09.12)

Following my request that the PHSO reconsider this, the position was upheld: 'You argue that the broader issues of governance, risk management and public confidence you raised with the SHA have not been investigated ... (as) the Chairman of the SHA told you ... they were not free-standing matters to be investigated' (Personal correspondence from PHSO, 31.01.2013). Framing and funnelling work in tandem. The SHA had appeared to frame my questions purely as a challenge to an individual, referring this to the AC to investigate, but then using its review as justification for rebuttal of all concerns. Personal and public issues were now presented as wholly intertwined. As this appeared to prevent an effective scrutiny of why the SHL contract failed, I sought a fuller explanation from the SHA.

Repudiation

By this time, with the impending abolition of the SHA, its Chair had been appointed to chair the newly created NHS Property Services (NHSPS), a company wholly owned by the Department of Health and established under the NHS re-organisation to take responsibility for buildings and estates previously managed by PCTs and SHAs. The appointment offers further insights into the role of social networks and hierarchies. A subsequent investigation of NHSPS by the National Audit Office noted, 'The Secretary of State appointed the chair of the company. The Department and the candidate himself told us that he was recommended for the role by the then chief executive of the NHS and a former permanent secretary of the Department, rather than being recruited through open competition' (National Audit Office 2014: 5).

The response to my question came from the lawyer, by now described as acting on behalf of NHSPS:

> You are not an investigator, regulator or statutory body and you have no standing from which to require anyone to co-operate with your lines of enquiry. None of these people are accountable to you ... I am in the process of drafting a Protection from Harassment Act letter to you regarding proceedings to seek an injunction against you. (Personal correspondence from NHSPS lawyer, 23.04.13)

Five months later, as I was pursuing requests for information disclosure through the Information Commissioner, complaints about me were submitted by the NHSPS Chair and a senior director of NHSPS to my Vice-Chancellor. Subject access requests, to the University and NHSPS revealed details. The complaint was sent to the Vice-Chancellor's office on 24th September 2013, soon after I submitted my complaint against DH to the ICO, when I sought an un-redacted version of Mr Howeson's letter to the Appointments Commission. I had learned of this letter through a disclosure to a previous FOIA request, as it was listed as one of the sources in the AC investigation. The email to the VC informs her that my concern:

> was originally the subject of an independent review by the Appointments Committee (*sic*). They found no substance to MS's concerns. Indeed it was highly critical of the way he had raised them. Given MS was dissatisfied with the outcome he asked the Parliamentary Ombudsman, and the Information Commissioner, to review his complaint. Again, they found no substance to MS's allegations ... (name redacted) suggested (name redacted) arrange a telephone call to Professor Purcell to discuss possible next steps. (SAR; email from NHSPS to the office of University of Plymouth Vice-Chancellor (UoP VC), 24.09.13. Disclosed by UoP)

On 1st October, the NHSPS director informs Mr Howeson and the lawyer that he has a telephone call arranged with the VC for the coming Friday, 'so will report back then' (SAR; email from NHSPS director to NHSPS Chair and lawyer, 01.10.13. Disclosed by UoP). Three days later, an email thanks the VC, 'for the opportunity to discuss this issue', to which the VC replied: 'Thank you for drawing me into your confidence on this difficult matter – I have already actioned a review of his email use in line with our IT policy. I shall call you to update as appropriate' (SAR; emails between NHSPS and UoP VC, 04.10.2013. Disclosed by UoP).

At the end of October, a letter from the VC to Mr Howeson refers to having received:

> your "private" email regarding concerns about one of the University's lecturers, Dr Mike Sheaff, relating to matters associated with one of his external non-executive positions. (Redacted section). Having drawn us in, it might be interpreted by others as an invitation for us to intervene in the dispute which I know you would agree would be entirely inappropriate. We fully appreciate your efforts here relate to your deep respect for our University and anything that might impact on our reputation with key stakeholders.' The letter concludes: 'It is our considered view that there should be no further written communication among us on this matter. I feel sure you will understand the sensitivities here given you are a valued friend and supporter of your alma mater. (SAR; Letter from UoP VC to Chair of NHSPS, 30.10.13. Disclosed by NHSPS)

Four years previously, Mr Howeson had received an honorary doctorate from the University. On 16th December, the VC wrote to the NHSPS director about his complaint: 'I wanted to update you on our investigation regarding the recent complaint against Dr Mike Sheaff relating to his correspondence with the now disbanded Strategic Health Authority ... We have now completed our complaints procedure and, while mindful of our commitment to the principle of academic freedom, have placed details of our investigation on his personnel file' (SAR; email from UoP VC to NHSPS, 16.12.13. Disclosed by UoP).

A threat of an injunction and complaints to my employer represented significant shifts in the style of response. Framing and funnelling had already obstructed meaningful investigation of the Secure Healthcare contract, and the role of the Department of Health, achieving a largely successful performance of clean-up work. Escalation coincided with my decision to adopt a more systematic approach to researching the SHL contract through FOIA requests.

Privacy, Reputation and Accountability

The chapter concludes with an example of how the complex balance between competing interests contributes to the framing of issues as 'public' or 'personal'. It concerns the letter written by the SHA Chair to the Appointments Commission, mentioned above. Having initially received a very heavily redacted version from DH in response to a FOIA request, I obtained a slightly more detailed version following an internal review. But this still provided very limited information, prompting my complaint to the Information Commissioner. DH's redactions were upheld, and the ICO noted in the Decision Notice: 'The DoH said whilst the redacted information relates to the data subject's public lives, disclosure into the public domain may cause damage to the professional reputation of the data subjects.' (*ICO Decision Notice FS50503556: para 17*). In my grounds of appeal to the Tribunal, I suggested, 'that expectations of data subjects should be reasonable, taking account of all the circumstances of a particular case. The public interest concerns the response of very senior NHS staff to concerns brought to their attention'. Having taken advice from counsel, the Information Commissioner responded:

> The Commissioner accepts that as the data subjects in this case occupy or occupied very senior positions in the NHS – they should have anticipated a greater level of scrutiny of and accountability for their actions. However, the Commissioner had to consider what the reasonable expectations of the data subjects were in relation to the information which was requested … As a consequence, even though the individuals all occupied senior positions, the Commissioner concluded that the disclosure of the third party personal data would be unfair and contrary to the first data protection principle. (In the matter of an appeal between Dr Michael Sheaff and The Information Commissioner|: Response on Behalf of the Information Commissioner, 20.012.14)

Included in the respondent's bundle for the hearing was a statement from the former SHA Chair urging non-disclose of the redacted sections, saying, 'I have discussed this with two colleagues involved in this correspondence. It's fair to say we clearly expect the Secretary of State to firmly protect us and our reputations in the proper execution of our duties as leaders within the NHS' (Statement submitted to Information Rights Tribunal, Sheaff and The Information Commissioner & The Department of Health, EA/2014/0005). In its judgment dismissing the appeal, the

Tribunal referred to, 'the entirely legitimate purposes of MS's quest for greater transparency and accountability', however, in applying its interpretation of the law, it noted: 'there is a general expectation that internal staff matters will remain confidential. We do not accept the distinction made by MS between disciplinary issues and other expressions of opinion as to staff members *nor the argument that public office holders are not entitled to the same protection of personal data as employees.* We find that all concerned reasonably expected that the matters referred to would remain confidential within a limited circle of senior personnel' (*Sheaff and The Information Commissioner & The Department of Health, EA/2014/0005: para. 23. emphasis added*).

The majority of redactions in the letter were under FOIA s40(2), concerning third-party personal information, but one bullet point was redacted under s40(1), i.e. my personal information. The Tribunal judgment noted, 'FOIA s.40(1) provides an absolute exemption for information of which the applicant (here MS) is the data subject. That is because the DPA 1998 s.7 makes provision for a subject access request, which is the appropriate route for disclosure. Accordingly, in so far as the letter contains the personal data of MS, the appeal must fail' (*Sheaff and The Information Commissioner & The Department of Health, EA/2014/0005: para. 11).*

A subject access request to DH seeking disclosure of this bullet-point was also refused. Acknowledging this was my personal data, DH explained its position:

> The DPA prevents us from disclosing to you any personal data which is not yours. It also prevents us from breaching any duty of confidentiality owed to any other individuals involved ... The first bullet point expresses a viewpoint held by another individual at the time of writing and therefore is also their personal data. The Department cannot disclose this without breaching the confidentiality of the individual concerned and consequently disclosure is refused. (Response from Department of Health to subject access request, 03.01.14)

Denial of access to personal data on the basis that, as an expression of opinion, it is also the personal data of the person holding it, extends ownership of personal data in ways that further stretches the boundary of privacy. It seemed to provide another route for those holding appropriate material, social and cultural resources to evade legitimate scrutiny and accountability.

But an immeasurably more serious illustration of a relationship between power, status, social networks and concealment came in early 2016, with the arrest of the former SHA Chair on allegations of historic sex offences, which he vehemently denied. Subsequently, he was found guilty on ten charges involving abuse of eight young men, while he was a Royal Navy officer, and later chief executive of a charity, Groundworks. The judge imposed a prison sentence of seven and a half years. Fifty-four character witnesses provided support for the defence, including an MP, an NHS Trust Chair, and many other senior figures (Turner 2017). Dismissing a subsequent appeal, the Court of Appeal commented on issues of public roles and private lives, noting how, 'the judge acknowledged the positive good character of the Appellant who had given years of service to the Royal Navy and to various charities and public works, and he had worked at the highest level in public bodies authorities and business. The references provided to the court were powerful'. However, 'the Appellant was in a position of some authority – a dominant position – over each victim', and the judgment continued:

> He has spent much of his life in public service, in the Royal Navy and then with charities and in public works. However, as the sentencing guidelines emphasise and as the judge indicated, that has to be balanced against the fact that he used his position in authority in the Navy and then Groundworks to commit these offences. That misuse of his position undermines the mitigation of his positively good character ... the Appellant engaged in a course of conduct over more than ten years involving eight victims in three different contexts, but over all of whom he had a significant position of authority by virtue of his rank as Commander in the Royal Navy or as a Senior Executive at Groundwork. His victims were far lower down the order. All the victims were, to that extent, vulnerable. (*R v Howeson, Court of Appeal, 26.10.18. EWCA Crim 2503*)

Constructions of boundaries between private and public lives involve protection of privacy but can also conceal and protect wrongdoing. Becker's concept of the 'hierarchy of credibility' looms large in situations where there can be a conflict over the disclosure and interpretation of information. The outcome of the former SHA Chair's trial caused me to reflect again on processes and practices contributing to the creation of socially credible accounts. As questions of considerable analytical, social and political importance, the final chapter considers the contested arena of private spaces and public issues, incorporating in later sections further reflection on my own experience.

References

Appointments Commission. (2011). *Review of the Appointment of xxxx as Chair of xxxx Trust*. Leeds: Appointments Commission.

Becker, H. (1967). Whose Side Are We On? *Social Problems, 14*(3), 234–247.

Bulmer, M. (1982). The Merits and Demerits of Covert Participant Observation. In M. Bulmer (Ed.), *Social Research Ethics: An Examination of the Merits of Covert Participant Observation* (pp. 217–251). New York: Holmes and Meier.

Costas, J., & Grey, C. (2016). *Secrecy at Work: The Hidden Architecture of Organizational Life*. Stanford: Stanford University Press.

den Heyer, G. (2011). New Public Management: A strategy for Democratic Police Reform in Transitioning and Developing Countries. *Policing: An International Journal of Police Strategies & Management, 34*(3), 419–433.

du Gay, P. (2008). Keyser Suze Elites: Market Populism and the Politics of International Change. *Sociological Review Monograph Series, 56*(1), 80–102.

Exton, R. (2008). The Entrepreneur: A New Breed of Health Service Leader? *Journal of Health Organization and Management, 22*(3), 208–222.

Friedman, N. L. (1990). Autobiographical Sociology. *The American Sociologist, 21*(1), 60–66.

Goffman, E. (1959/1990). *The Presentation of Self in Everyday Life*. London: Penguin.

Gould, M. (2009, November 18). An Ill Wind Blows for Social Enterprise. *The Guardian*.

Health Services Journal. (2007, February 15). After Eden, Things Look Rosy in the Social Enterprise Garden. *Health Service Journal*. https://www.hsj.co.uk/news/after-eden-things-look-rosy-in-the-social-enterprise-garden/1640.article

Her Majesty's Inspector of Prisons (HMIP). (2004). *Report on an Announced Inspection of HMP Wandsworth 17–21 May 2004 by HM Chief Inspector of Prisons*. London: HMIP.

Her Majesty's Inspector of Prisons. (2006). *Report on a Full Follow-Up Inspection of HMP Wandsworth 10–14 July 2006 by HM Chief Inspector of Prisons*. London: HMIP.

Her Majesty's Inspectors of Prisons. (2009). *Report of an Announced Inspection of HMP Wandsworth (1–5 June 2009) by HM Chief Inspector of Prisons*. London: HMIP.

Jones, L., & Exworthy, M. (2015). Framing in Policy Processes: A Case Study from Hospital Planning in the National Health Service in England. *Social Science and Medicine, 124*(2015), 196–204.

Morgan, G. (1986). *Images of Organization*. Beverley Hills: Sage.

National Audit Office. (2014). *Memorandum for the House of Commons Health Committee: Investigation into NHS Property Services Ltd*. London: National Audit Office.

NHS London Audit Consortium. (2010). *Secure Healthcare*. London: NHS London Audit Consortium.

NHS Wandsworth. (2009). *Prison Healthcare Services – Insolvency of Secure Healthcare Limited PCT Review*. London: NHS Wandsworth.

Plummer, K. (2001). *Documents of Life 2*. London: SAGE Publications.

Royal College of Nursing. (2007, February). *Policy Briefing: Social Enterprise Update*. London: RCN.

Secretary of State for Health. (2006). *Our Health, Our Care, Our Say: A New Direction for Community Services*. London: HMSO.

Secure Healthcare Ltd. (2009a). *Annual Return and Accounts*. London: Secure Healthcare.

Secure Healthcare Ltd. (2009b, September 9). *Report to SHL Board of Directors*. London: Meeting.

Shaw, E. (2004). What Matters Is What Works: The Third Way and the Case of the Private Finance Initiative. In S. Hale, W. Leggett, & L. Martell (Eds.), *The Third Way and Beyond: Criticisms, Futures, Alternatives* (pp. 64–82). Manchester: Manchester University Press.

Sheaff, M. (1988). NHS Ancillary Services and Competitive Tendering. *Industrial Relations Journal, 19*(2), 93–105.

Shore, C., & Wright, S. (1997). *Anthropology of Policy: Perspectives on Governance and Power*. London: Routledge.

Simonet, D. (2011). The New Public Management Theory and the Reform of European Health Care Systems: An International Comparative Perspective. *International Journal of Public Administration, 34*(12), 815–826.

South West London & St George's NHS Mental Health Trust (SWL&SG). (2011). *Secure Healthcare: Report to Audit Committee*. SWL&SG.

Stanley, L. (1993). On Auto/Biography in Sociology. *Sociology, 27*(1), 41–52.

Taylor, A. (2007, July 2). Prison Health Contract Goes to Secure Healthcare. *Community Care*.

Tribal Newchurch. (2009). *Social Enterprise Pathfinder Programme Evaluation Report 4 – Final Report*. London.

Turner, C. (2017, December 22). The High Profile People That Supported Charles Howeson During His Trial. *Plymouth Herald*. https://www.plymouthherald.co.uk/news/plymouth-news/high-profile-people-supported-charles-968857

Vaughan, D. (1999). The Dark Side of Organizations: Mistake, Misconduct and Disaster. *Annual Review of Sociology, 25*, 271–305.

Wandsworth PCT (2009). *Minutes of Wandsworth PCT Community Services Board*, 17 November 2009. London: Wandsworth PCT.

Wandsworth PCT (2010). *Minutes of Wandsworth PCT Community Services Board*, 19 January 2010. London: Wandsworth PCT.

CHAPTER 6

Trust, Transparency and Privacy

Abstracts The chapter demonstrates changing UK government attitudes towards freedom of information through two examples of its use of a veto of information disclosure. These concerned legal advice on the 2003 Iraq war and risk assessments of the 2011 NHS reforms. Under governments of different political persuasion, both involved claims that a 'private space' is needed for government deliberations. A discussion on 'making the private public' uses examples from feminist challenges to public/private boundaries, and ways professional work has been subject to greater scrutiny and monitoring. A discussion on implications for those engaged in researching decision-making includes Sheaff's own reflection on his position in the research described in Chap. 5. Sheaff concludes by arguing a role for social research in addressing issues of secrecy, accountability and justice.

Keywords Transparency • Feminism • Chilling-effect • Dark secrets • Public sociology

Private Spaces and Public Issues

Following his paean to freedom of information in the 1997 White Paper, Tony Blair's views changed dramatically, expressed in his autobiography:

> Freedom of Information. Three harmless words. I look at those words as I write them, and feel like shaking my head till it drops off my shoulders. You

M. Sheaff, *Secrecy, Privacy and Accountability*,
https://doi.org/10.1007/978-3-030-11686-6_6

> idiot. You naive, foolish, irresponsible nincompoop. There is really no description of stupidity, no matter how vivid, that is adequate. I quake at the imbecility of it. Once I appreciated the full enormity of the blunder, I used to say – more than a little unfairly – to any civil servant who would listen: Where was Sir Humphrey when I needed him? We had legislated in the first throes of power. How could you, knowing what you know have allowed us to do such a thing so utterly undermining of sensible government? (Blair 2010: 516)

Acknowledging his earlier commitment to freedom of information legislation, Tony Blair has since pointed out, 'but, that was before the experience of Government' (Blair 2012). Writing to the Chair of the Justice Committee conducting Post-legislative scrutiny of the Freedom of information Act, Tony Blair explains why he believes 'the FOI Act was a mistake'. In summary, he suggests 'Government requires a certain degree of confidentiality to work effectively.' He notes the Act provides exemptions, but expresses concern that disclosure has gone beyond the intention of the legislation, claiming, 'the original idea was to make available the facts behind the decisions, not the confidential policy debate around those decisions. In reality, publication now goes way beyond that with the public interest tests giving a big impulsion in the direction of publication' (Blair 2012).

Tony Blair asserts this constrains the creation and maintenance of records about complex and difficult issues. He goes on to suggest that openness has unintended consequences through fettering private discussion: 'I am not at all sure that the Act has really achieved its goal of greater transparency … if people know that what they are saying is going to be published, they will be less frank and open in how they express themselves.' The purpose of the legislation was, he suggests, 'not to open such frank discussion to public view', but 'to allow issues to be better debated; to permit people to access information about themselves held by Government; and to encourage the system to be more accountable'. He adds, 'I thought the Act would benefit the public. Actually I think it has really tilted the scales on various contentious issues toward the media' (Blair 2012).

Claims that transparency might distort the character of private discussions between public officials have been central to use of the ministerial veto to overrule instructions to disclose material. An important example came in response to a request for disclosure of Cabinet minutes and meeting records from March 2003 concerning legal advice from the Attorney General on military action against Iraq. The Cabinet Office refused disclosure on public interest grounds, arguing the need for confidentiality surrounding policy development and ministerial communications. Acknowledging these provided potential grounds for non-disclosure, the Information Commissioner nevertheless rejected this view. Referring to 'the gravity and controversial nature of the decision to go to war', and the, 'public interest in transparency given the controversy surrounding the Attorney General's legal advice on the legality of the military action', the Information Commissioner, 'did not consider that the information in the public domain sufficiently enabled the public to scrutinise the manner in which the decision was taken and took the view that disclosure of the Minutes was necessary to understand that decision more fully' (Information Commissioner 2009: 8).

The Cabinet Office appealed to the Tribunal, which by 2–1 majority decided that on balance the public interest favoured disclosure of the minutes. The Tribunal described this as an: 'an exceptional case, the circumstances of which brought together a combination of factors that were so important that, in combination, they created very powerful public interest reasons why disclosure was in the public interest' (Information Commissioner 2009: 11). On 23 February 2009, Jack Straw, Secretary of State for Justice, issued a 'veto' certificate under section 53(2) of the Act, overruling this decision. The core of his argument was that Cabinet discussions need the protection of a 'private space' to allow free and frank debate: 'Dialogue must be fearless. Ministers must have the confidence to challenge each other in private ... To permit the commissioner's and the tribunal's view of the public interest to prevail would, in my judgement, risk serious damage to Cabinet government – an essential principle of British parliamentary democracy' (Ministry of Justice 2009).

Two years later, a similar argument was again applied to use of the ministerial veto, preventing the release of documents concerning the Coalition Government's NHS re-organisation described in Chap. 5. Disclosure of a Transitional Risk Register (TRR), created as part of DH's risk assessment of the proposed changes, was refused on the grounds that, 'disclosure would or would be likely to inhibit the free and frank provision of advice'. As this is a qualified exemption subject to a 'public interest' test, the applicant requested an internal review. DH maintained its refusal, but changed the justification, now stating the information was exempt from disclosure as it was concerned with the formulation and development of government policy. Also a qualified exemption, DH continued its claim that the public interest favoured non-disclosure.

The applicant complained to the Information Commissioner, arguing there was an important public interest at issue, as disclosure would allow greater scrutiny of the government's plans. In response, DH claimed disclosure would jeopardise success of the policy through inhibiting frank discussion. Concluding the arguments were finely balanced, the ICO judged the information should be disclosed:

> there is a very strong public interest in disclosure of the information, given the significant change to the structure of the health service the government's policies on the modernisation will bring. There has also been widespread public debate amongst the general public, commentators, experts and those who work in the NHS … Disclosure would significantly aid public understanding of the risks related to the proposed reforms and it would also inform participation in the debate about the reforms. (*ICO DN FS50390786: para 31*)

DH appealed the decision to the Information Tribunal, which took evidence from a former Cabinet Secretary and the DH Permanent Secretary who endorsed the view that disclosure would inhibit thinking and consequently damage sound policymaking. The Tribunal accepted, 'a safe space is required for government to formulate and develop policy', but argued the significance of this would change over time (para 59). Rejecting the evidence from the senior civil servants, the Tribunal concluded, 'there was no actual evidence of such an effect' (para 66), and noted research by the Constitution Unit at University College London that found little evidence that FOIA has what is described as a 'chilling effect' on discussion. This point is made clearly in the Unit's end of award report for an ESRC-funded project:

> FOI has not caused a 'chilling effect' on frank advice and deliberation, or on the quality of government records. The myth persists, but convincing evidence proved hard to find. There was no evidence of any decline in the quality of official advice. Ministers may resort to 'sofa government', and there is deterioration in the quality of government records; but there is no evidence to link this to FOI. Sofa government results from ministerial preferences and behaviour. The deterioration in government records results from starving the record keeping function of resources. Given so few specific FOI examples, we concluded the chilling effect to be a myth, albeit a pervasive one. (Hazell and Worthy 2009: 6)

In the case of the DH risk register, the Tribunal concluded the public interest justified disclosure:

> the NHS reforms were introduced in an exceptional way. There was no indication prior to the White Paper that such wide ranging reforms were being considered. The White Paper was published without prior consultation. It was published within a very short period after the Coalition Government came into power. It was unexpected. Consultation took place afterwards over what appears to us a very short period considering the extent of the proposed reforms ... Even more significantly the Government decided to press ahead with some of the policies even before laying a Bill before Parliament.' (para 85) ... We find the weight we give to the need for transparency and accountability in the circumstances of this case to be very weighty indeed. (para 89)

This decision was overruled by the Secretary of State for Health three days later, who claimed, 'there was a significant risk' that 'disclosure of the TRR at this time would in fact have distorted debate and understanding' (Information Commissioner 2012: 28). The Information Commissioner's subsequent report to Parliament noted: 'The previous three occasions on which the veto has been exercised related to the disclosure of Cabinet material under FOIA. The Commissioner would wish to record his concern that the exercise of the veto in this case extends its use into other areas of the policy process. It represents a departure from the position adopted in the Statement of Policy and therefore marks a significant step in the Government's approach to freedom of information' (Information Commissioner 2012: 19–20).

The Constitutional Reform and Governance Act 2010, passed just before the 2010 general election, introduced two amendments to exemptions in FOIA. These made Cabinet papers subject to an absolute exemption for twenty years, and exemptions relevant to 'communications with the Royal Household' were made absolute. The latter arose from a long-running legal dispute, ending in the Supreme Court, on use of the ministerial veto in resisting disclosure of correspondence from HRH Prince Charles. The Campaign for Freedom of Information expressed 'serious concern' when the new exemptions were first proposed (Campaign for Freedom of Information 2009), but the government claimed existing safeguards, 'are insufficiently robust to protect our current constitutional arrangements, and need changing' (Rosenbaum 2009). Illustrating increasing restrictions on disclosure, these examples provide a context for placing the increased reliance on exempting ‘personal information’ from disclosure in the context of other debates involving contested boundaries between private and public. Two very different examples are used. The first draws upon feminist challenges to dominant definitions of the ‘private’, and the second involves increasing public scrutiny of professional practice, illustrated with reference to social work.

Making the Private Public

This section returns to the issue of trust through considering other examples of constructions of the private/public distinction. Government claims about a damaging ‘chilling effect’, should private discussion be disclosed appear unfounded, but a more legitimate concern could be that FOIA disclosures contribute to declining public trust in those in authority, especially politicians. Opinion poll data from 1994 and 2013 identified 52% in each year, saying they believed MPs put their own interests first. At the height of the expenses scandal, the proportion rose to 62%. Between 2006 and 2009, the proportion who do not trust MPs in general to tell the truth increased from 60% to 76%, but was still as high as 72% in 2013 (Ipsos/MORI, *Trust in MP’s*, 13th June 2013).

From its own research, the UCL Constitution Unit concludes that although FOI has made, ‘British government more transparent and accountable’, it has not achieved other objectives of increasing public participation, improving public understanding of government decision-making, or increasing trust in government. It adds, ‘if anything trust has decreased, especially as a result of the MPs’ expenses scandal’ (UCL Constitution Unit 2016). As described in Chap. 2, the House of Commons had claimed details of expenses were the personal information of individual MPs and consequently exempt from disclosure. Once un-redacted information was released through leaks to the *Daily Telegraph*, this claim generated widespread perception of a deceitful concealment of wrongdoing. But in other cases, ‘personal information’ is protected when, what is at issue is not wrongdoing, or corruption, but mistake, misunderstanding, inattention to detail, or the like. Seen as potentially damaging to reputation and thus an unjustified intrusion into privacy, such information gains protection. As noted, there has been a steady rise in the proportion of disclosure refusals by government departments on the grounds that information is ‘personal’.

A recent FOIA request by the satirical magazine, *Private Eye*, illustrates consequences. The request was prompted by mention in the government's hospitality 'transparency data' of the attendance by Alex Chisholm, permanent secretary at the Department for Business, Energy and Industrial Strategy, at a dinner hosted by Lord Mandelson. The response disclosed Lord Mandelson's invitation, in which he explained, 'I periodically invite people from business and elsewhere to meet for dinner and to discuss the world and to share views. There is no agenda, simply an opportunity for a small group of smart and engaging individuals to meet and talk.' Names of other attendees were redacted, on the grounds this was 'personal data'. *Private Eye* comment, 'So while the public *is* allowed to know that Chisholm had no special "dietary requirements" and he was so "keen" to attend the 14 March dinner he arranged to "leave early" from an earlier engagement, no one is allowed to know who was bending his ears or picking his brains' (HP Sauce, *Private Eye*, No 1477: 9). Refusal to disclose this type of information may needlessly contribute to a suspicion that something is amiss.

Conflict over the construction of the public-private boundaries has been a feature in many other debates. One of the most notable comes from feminist challenges. Landes (1998) describes how feminism, 'upset the firm divisions between public and private matters' (Landes 1998: 2) evident in dominant political discourses, and also how the line between the two is, 'constantly being renegotiated' (Landes 1998: 3). Benhabib illustrates this in discussing the formation of modern 'public spaces' in contrast to those of ancient society. In modern times, she argued:

> public space is essentially porous; neither access to it nor its agenda of debate can be predefined by criteria of moral and political homogeneity. With the entry of every new group into the public space of politics after the French and American revolutions, the scope of the public gets extended. The emancipation of workers made property relations into a public-political issue; the emancipation of women has meant that the family and the so-called private sphere become political issues ... The struggle over what gets included in the public agenda is itself a struggle for justice and freedom. (Benhabib 1992: 94)

> As with any modern liberation movement, the contemporary women's movement is making what were hitherto considered "private" matters of the good life into "public" issues of justice by thematizing the asymmetrical power relations on which the sexual division of labor between the genders has rested. In this process, the line between the private and the public,

> between issues of justice and matters of the good life is being renegotiated. (Benhabib 1992: 109)

Such negotiations take place within unequal social relationships. Fraser (1998) describes a struggle in 1991 over George Bush's Supreme Court nomination of a black conservative, Clarence Thomas. Subject to allegations from a former female assistant of sexual harassment, Thomas refused to address questions he contended breached his privacy. In one Senate hearing he responded:

> I am … not here to put my private life on display for prurient interests or other reasons. I will not allow this committee or anyone else to probe into my private life … I will not provide the rope for my own lynching or for further humiliation. I am not going to engage in discussions nor will I submit to roving questions about what goes on in the most intimate parts of my private life, or the sanctity of my bedroom. These are the most intimate parts of my privacy, and they will remain just that, private. (Quoted in Fraser 1998: 321)

Fraser describes how public attention shifted to the motives of Anita Hill, who had made the allegations. 'Hill also sought to define and defend her privacy but was less successful than Thomas. Although she sought to keep the focus on her complaint and on the evidence that corroborated it, the principal focus soon became *her* character' (Fraser 1998: 322). Fraser's argument is that conflicting claims concerning the construction of an issue as private or public do not take place in a social vacuum. Not only is the boundary between public and private a contested one, when conflicts about privacy emerge, 'some have more power than others to draw and defend the line' (Fraser 1998: 334).

A different example of the construction of the public/private boundary comes from increasing scrutiny of professional work, illustrated with the example of child social work. As feminists argued, the family can be a space where public issues, of inequality, neglect and abuse, are paramount, sometimes bringing tragic consequences. The 1985 report commissioned by the London Borough of Brent into the death of Jasmine Beckford the previous year includes a comment from an area director of social services at the time of the inquiry into the death of Maria Colwell in 1973. She wrote how the media and public attention, 'was beyond our experience, because until that time nothing had been more private than social work'

(Blom-Cooper 1985: 12). Commenting on this expression, the inquiry notes: 'A whole generation of social workers, senior social workers, area managers and directors of Social Services were suddenly brought face to face with the fact that they were publicly accountable for their actions' (Blom-Cooper 1985: 12). A view that the social workers/client relationship was very different to the doctor/patient relationship gave rise to a particular framing of the character of professionalism in social work: 'we are strongly of the view that social work can, in fact, be defined *only* in terms of the functions required of its practitioners by their employing agency operating within a statutory framework' (Blom-Cooper 1985: 12, emphasis in original). Through a series of investigations following subsequent tragedies, a particular style of transparency developed, demanding attention to policies, protocols and inspections. However, by 2010, Professor Eileen Munroe described a need:

> to reform the child protection system from being over-bureaucratised and concerned with compliance to one that keeps a focus on children, checking whether they are being effectively helped, and adapting when problems are identified. A move from a compliance to a learning culture will require those working in child protection to be given more scope to exercise professional judgment in deciding how best to help children and their families. It will require more determined and robust management at the front line to support the development of professional confidence. (Munroe 2011: 5)

Many writers have noted how accountability and transparency mechanisms introduced in professional practice involve increased surveillance and managerial control. Eliot Freidson, whose early work highlighted the power and autonomy of the US medical profession (Freidson 1970a, b), was by the later part of his life observing how:

> enthusiasm for these (neoliberal) ideologies during the past few decades has seriously weakened the appeal of the professional ideology … The economically self-interested actions of the profession and its failure to undertake responsibility for assuring the quality of its members work weakened its claims and appeared to confirm the truth of the assumptions of consumerism and managerialism. (Freidson 2001: 190)

As mentioned previously, in the wake of the public inquiry into Mid Staffs Hospital, a significant source of grievance among relatives of former patients was that although action was taken against some nursing staff, including removal from the professional register, no equivalent sanctions were applied to those in senior executive and non-executive positions. Not only has public trust in politicians declined; there is also an apparently widespread perception that others in authority can escape scrutiny and accountability. In this context, and given the flexibility attaching to the construction of privacy rights, the distinctively neoliberal models of privacy and transparency warrant close attention.

Concepts of privacy, secrecy, transparency and accountability are examples of 'essentially contested concepts' (Gallie 1956). In Europe, this has given rise to conflicts within the framework of different Articles in the European Convention on Human Rights, notably between the right to a private life and a right to freedom of expression. Several accounts of the emergence of Article 8 of the Convention, the right to a private life, refer to the influence of conservative thinking, following the end of the Second World War, in response to fears of increased state control. For some, the election of the 1945 Labour Government meant, 'the British executive was, in their view, increasingly ready to deny "personal rights" in the name of protecting economic and social rights' (Duranti 2012: 362). Referring to a description of the history of human rights as 'the history of conflict' (Duranti 2012: 363), Duranti notes 'Churchill had eliminated a reference in an early draft to "those fundamental human and personal rights" ... Instead he had favoured using the phrase "those fundamental personal rights and liberties"' Duranti 2012: 367). Deliberately departing from the broader range of rights established in the Universal Declaration, in Duranti's interpretation, classical liberalism was 'the formative ideational framework for European human rights law' (Duranti 2012: 377).

While this framework shaped development of UK law, doubts have been expressed about the interpretation given to it by the Information Commissioner. For example, Julian Farrand QC has argued the ICO guidance places too much emphasis on protection of personal data. Farrand suggests the ICO puts a consideration of, 'possible consequences of disclosure for the individual and his or her reasonable expectations ... before balancing legitimate interests in access to information against the privacy rights of data subjects'. Arguing this effectively overrides parliament's 'balancing intention' (Farrand 2016: 385), Farrand concludes the, 'guidance offered is significantly but wrongly weighted in favour of privacy and against freedom of information. This weighting-bias may partly explain the perceived over-reliance on this exemption noted in the MoJ's Post-Legislative Assessment' (Farrand 2016: 392).

Sociological interest in human rights has been described as consistent with a 'normative turn' within the discipline, marking, 'a shift in sociology, away from scientism (the conception of the analyst as a neutral and objective observer) and the idea that relatively autonomous and rational individuals competitively pursue their interests' (Blau and Moncada 2009: 507–598). A considerable sociological tradition does not conform to this description, but it highlights the importance of testing boundaries in the access of information. These remain highly contested, illustrated in a 2016 case heard by the European Court of Human Rights in which the UK government intervened to urge rejection of the view freedom of expression under Article 10 extends to access to information:

> the intervening Government submitted that in previous cases where the Court had found it necessary to update its case-law, this had been to ensure that it reflected contemporary social attitudes. No such need existed in the case of freedom of information. If the Court were to recognise a right of access to information held by the State, this would far exceed the legitimate interpretation of the Convention and would amount to judicial legislation. (*Magyar Helsinski Bizottsag v Hungary 2016*)

The case involved access to information on public lawyers acting for police departments in Hungary, sought by a non-governmental organisation, and the Court's judgment adopted a more nuanced approach than that urged by the UK government, explaining that:

> the Court considers that an important consideration is whether the person seeking access to the information in question does so with a view to informing the public in the capacity of a public "watchdog". This does not mean, however, that a right of access to information ought to apply exclusively to NGOs and the press ... a high level of protection also extends to academic researchers and authors of literature on matters of public concern. (*Magyar Helsinski Bizottsag v Hungary 2016*)

Developments in case law of this type suggest further opportunities for researchers to utilise freedom of information requests, a theme I return to in the next section, incorporating personal reflections on my own experiences, especially in researching an example of 'clean-up work'.

Personal Troubles and Public Issues

In her account of the *Challenger* disaster, Vaughan describes the role of communication failings between NASA teams (structural secrecy), but also notes, 'after the disaster, it appeared that Marshall managers intentionally concealed information' (Vaughan 1996: 238). Vaughan calls upon us not to collude in dominant but misleading accounts of organisational failure, even inadvertently:

> To a great extent, we are unwitting participants because without extraordinary expenditure of time and energy we cannot get beyond appearances. But we are also complicitous, for we bring to our interpretations of public failures a wish to blame, a penchant for psychological explanations, an inability to identify the structural and cultural causes, and a need for a straightforward, simple answer that can be quickly grasped. But the answer is seldom simple. Even when our hindsight is clear and we acknowledge the players omitted from the media spotlight, as long as we see organizational failures as the result of individual actions our strategies for control will be ineffective, and dangerously so. (Vaughan 1996: 392–393)

This plea has moral and analytical dimensions. To help address the former, I consider my own subjectivity in exploring the content of the 'clean-up work'. This is set within a framework that draws upon the work of Brewer (1984, 2004 and 2005), and in a different way, Frank (2013). Brewer relates a letter from C. Wright Mills to Miliband in 1957, describing his approach to dealing with criticism: 'I don't think it worthwhile to waste energy about it in small ways: analyze the world and locate them as a piece of shit within it' (Mills, in Brewer 2004: 331). This, suggests Brewer, 'rendered biography into sociology. In Mills's view it was the relationship between sociology and biography that helped to make sociology distinctive' (Brewer 2004: 331). Brewer describes how *The Sociological Imagination* emerged when Mills was in Europe, away from the USA, giving him a detachment allowing reflection, providing, 'a biographical space in which Mills could stand momentarily outside the discipline in the USA and envisage his contribution to it'. But alongside this, 'his deteriorating relations with the sociological establishment afforded the sense of personal hurt and anger that encouraged the desire to draw together his previous methodological statements and elaborate his vision for the discipline' (Brewer 2004: 323).

Drawing no other comparison, I too felt a sense of personal hurt and anger. I had a long relationship with the NHS, not only through a decade as a Non-Executive Director but also for seven years as an employee, when I was active as a trade union representative, and for a time a member of a health authority and a community health council. Having published research concerning the NHS, with much of my teaching having been with students of nursing, medicine and other health professions, I struggled when finding myself portrayed as promoting unfounded allegations. Later, as I reflected on this, immersing myself in material covering almost four years, I was drawn to a framework developed in an entirely different context, that of chronic illness. Frank (2013) uses the term 'narrative wreckage' to discuss the impact of chronic illness, involving a loss of the 'destination and map' that previously guided the person's life: ill people have to learn 'to think differently' (Frank 2013: 1). He outlines three narratives as responses. The first is the restitution narrative: 'yesterday I was healthy, today I'm sick, but tomorrow I'll be healthy again' (Frank 2013: 77). Within the context of illness and health, 'behind the restitution narrative is medicine' (Frank 2013: 83). In my own case, this was a period when I believed that concerns I raised would ultimately be acknowledged if I followed the appropriate procedures. This did not happen.

Frank's second narrative, the chaos narrative, is presented as the opposite to the restitution narrative: 'its plot imagines life never getting better. Stories are chaotic in their absence of narrative order' (Frank 2013: 97):

> The teller of chaos stories is, pre-eminently, the wounded storyteller, but those who are truly *living* the chaos cannot tell in words. To turn the chaos into a verbal story is to have some reflective grasp of it ... The person living the chaos story has no distance form her life and no reflective grasp on it. Lived chaos makes reflection, and consequently storytelling, impossible. (Frank 2013: 98, emphasis in original)

I felt something of this when receiving the threat of an injunction. Expectations that my concerns would be acknowledged by those in positions of authority were torn to shreds. I appreciate now how I turned to something analogous to what Franks describes as the 'quest narrative':

> quest stories meet suffering head on; they accept illness and seek to use it. Illness is the occasion of a journey that becomes a quest ... (Frank 2013: 115). The quest narrative recognizes ill people as responsible moral agents whose primary action is witness; its stories are necessary to restore the moral

> agency that other stories sacrifice. (Frank 2013: 134). Becoming a witness assumes a responsibility for telling what happened. The witness offers testimony to a truth that is generally unrecognized or suppressed. (Frank 2013: 137)

So my turn to a research focus was generated by more than an interest in exploring opportunities for using FOIA in research. Increasingly, this fascination grew, but it would be wrong not to acknowledge moral and emotional dimensions. I made contact with whistleblowers, becoming more aware that my experience was very far from an isolated one. As further information was disclosed by different organisations about the SHL contract, it became clear that, from a very early stage, there were significant problems that no-one addressed or even acknowledged. Three features struck me. First, organisational boundaries and divisions of responsibility meant there was no overall view of these problems as a whole. But just as important were the shared meanings and enthusiasm of those involved, obscuring a clearer vision and creating 'cognitive traps' (Morgan 1986). Secondly, when the collapse did occur, there was no acceptance of responsibility by those promoting the initiative at senior levels, and the DH-commissioned evaluation of the pathfinder programme included no discussion of this contract. Thirdly, a consequence was that nothing existed in the public domain to suggest a deeper problem, allowing investigations into my concerns to reinforce confidence in processes and practices. Misleading and inaccurate statements were not a consequence of insincerity, but reflected the accounts described in the publicly available records. Analogous to the idea of the creation of 'cognitive traps' through shared assumptions, the credibility of subsequent documentary records shape interpretations.

Taking responsibility as a researcher in these circumstances also requires recognition of the risks of imbalanced selectivity when looking back on experiences. The danger of ex post facto rationalisation in oral history is discussed by Brewer (1984) in a study of former members of the British Union of Fascists (BUF). Brewer draws upon the social phenomenology of Schutz, and his attention to, 'actors'' use of shared and publicly understood common-sense typifications. Hence the life-world has a dialectic character – part constructed by us on the basis of our personal biography, and part given to us in the form of public common-sense knowledge' (Brewer 1984: 745). This provides further insight into Frank's chaos narrative, as expectations of the role of formal complaints processes, based on the publicly understood common-sense knowledge, foundered on the rocks of lived experience. Despite limits of all autobiographical accounts, 'the full richness of any conscious experience is only available to the particular individual experiencing it' (Brewer 1984: 754). As I developed direct contact with whistleblowers, and read the accounts of others, I formed the view that my own experience had sociological value. Elsewhere, Brewer has written of the formation of C. Wright Mills' view that, 'the public role of sociology was to facilitate ordinary people to make sense of the social condition by showing how their personal troubles both impacted on and were impacted by public issues. Mills's vision for sociology can be understood as an autobiographical comment on the collapse of the public-private binary in his own life' (Brewer 2005: 674).

Secrecy, Accountability and Justice

'Public and private are categories that bleed into each other ... Just as public and private are essentially contested concepts, implicating us in competing normative frameworks, so is politics' (Elshtain 1997: 167–168). Discussing the slogan, 'the personal is political', Elshtain argues the continuing relevance of a distinction as, 'the rules of conduct which flow out of private relationships – intimacy, fidelity, self-disclosure – are not altogether transferable to public relationships where different criteria, including the capacity for provisional alliances – no permanent enemies; no permanent friends – are required' (Elshtain 1997: 180). This point is an important one, but its meaning needs continual reassessment in changing social and political circumstances. Increasing levels of mistrust of those in authority, and the rise of populist movements, reflect, at least in part, a perception that those 'in charge' act dishonestly, motivated solely by self-interest. The rise of populism, associated by Mouffe as a, 'crisis of the neoliberal hegemonic formation', is contrasted with an earlier, 'crisis of the social-democratic hegemonic formation established during the post-war years' (Mouffe 2018: 1–3). Referring to the 1985 book she co-wrote with Laclau, *Hegemony and Socialist Strategy*, Mouffe (2018) writes:

> We asserted that, in democratic societies, further crucial democratic advances could be carried out through a critical engagement with the existing institutions ... The 'radical and plural democracy' that we advocated can therefore be conceived as a radicalization of the existing democratic institutions, with the result that the principles of liberty and equality become effective in an

> increasing number of social relations … left populism seeks the establishment of a new hegemonic order within the constitutional liberal-democratic framework … Its objective is … to re-establish the articulation between liberalism and democracy that has been disavowed by neoliberalism, putting democratic values in the leading role. (Mouffe 2018: 39–45)

The exercise of secrecy by power-holders has long been an issue for social analysis. Writing in 1843, challenging Hegel's comments on mechanisms for the accountability of the state, Marx highlighted the correspondence between hierarchy and secrecy:

> The general spirit of the bureaucracy is the secret, the mystery, preserved inwardly by means of the hierarchy and externally as a closed corporation. To make public the mind and the disposition of the state appears therefore to the bureaucracy as a betrayal of its mystery. Accordingly authority is the principle of its knowledge and being, and the deification of authority is its mentality. (Marx 1843: 45)

Subsequent democratic reforms brought substantial change, but in 1914, when the German Social Democratic Party gained the largest number of seats in federal elections, Weber observed:

> 'Every bureaucracy seeks to increase the superiority of the professionally informed by keeping their knowledge and intentions secret. Bureaucratic administration always tends to be an administration of 'secret sessions'; in so far as it can, it hides its knowledge and actions from criticism … The official statistics of Prussia, in general, make public only what cannot do any harm to the intentions of the power-wielding bureaucracy ….
>
> The concept of the 'official secret' is the specific invention of the bureaucracy, and nothing is so fanatically defended by the bureaucracy as this attitude, which cannot be substantially justified beyond … specifically qualified areas. In facing a parliament, the bureaucracy, out of a sure power instinct, fights every attempt of the parliament to gain knowledge by means of its own experts or from interest groups. The so-called right of parliamentary investigation is one of the means by which parliament seeks such knowledge. Bureaucracy naturally welcomes a poorly informed and hence a powerless parliament – at least in so far as ignorance somehow agrees with the bureaucracy's interests.' (Max Weber 1914, in Gerth and Mills 1946)

Protection of private spaces is important, and not only for close, intimate relationships. There will be many circumstances, where those in positions of authority and leadership require confidentiality. But boundaries claimed for this require constant interrogation. One aim of research in this area is to find ways of, 'lifting the veils that obscure or hide what is going on. The task of scientific study is to lift the veils that cover the area of group life that one proposes to study … The veils are lifted by getting close to the area and by digging deep into it through careful study' (Blumer 1969: 39–47). Greater use of FOIA in social research offers a route to developing empirical material for exploring issues around the role of elites, hierarchies, and ways in which power is exercised, as well as the performance of 'clean-up work'. This can contribute to an analysis of what Lukes described as the second-face of power, which limits, 'the scope of the political process to public consideration of only those issues which are comparatively innocuous' (Bachrach and Baratz 1962: 948). One feature of this, illustrated in the case study, can be a failure to match in practice the idealised image of the 'enterprising self'. At times concealment may extend to what Goffman referred to as 'dark secrets': 'facts about a team which it knows and conceals and which are incompatible with the image of self that the team attempts to maintain before its audience … The audience must not acquire destructive information about the situation that is being defined for them' (Goffman 1959/1990: 141). Rather than concealing failure, it is perhaps the unrealistic image that needs rethinking.

The increasing use of s40 to exempt disclosure of 'personal information' in response to FOIA requests needs challenging. Personal privacy is important, and risks of 'scape-goating' are real. But a denial of transparency can result in responsibility for organisational failure being attributed to those at the operational 'front line'. Binary divisions between transparency and secrecy, as with public and private, are too simplistic. Questioning approaches to extending transparency in opposition to secrecy, Birchall instead advocates, 'working with the tension between these terms rather than responding to the dyad as a choice' (Birchall 2011: 7). I would go further in making the case for greater transparency, in large part because of increasing levels of public mistrust. Transparency in itself is not a solution, but it can assist analysis and debate. We need a better understanding of the interplay between individuals and organisations when things go wrong, including the role of shared assumptions, opinions and beliefs. These cannot meaningfully be described as purely 'private'. The issues themselves are not new, but how they are framed present new challenges. It is difficult to imagine a contemporary report delivering the sort of judgments on individual responsibility presented by the Aberfan inquiry. Much has changed since then, but there is a paradox that we live in an age when the importance of personal responsibility is proclaimed, yet it appears harder to trace that of those in authority.

We need to constantly rethink academic and moral responsibilities within our own times. As Durkheim observed in 1908, 'writers and scholars are citizens; it is thus evident that they have the strict duty to participate in public life' (cited in Cladis 1995: 187). Mills carried this idea forward in the period after the Second World War in his encouragement through the sociological imagination to, 'grasp history and biography and the relations between the two within society ... Perhaps the most fruitful distinction with which the sociological imagination works is between the "personal troubles of milieu" and the "public issues of social structure"' (Mills 1959). It is a theme continued by Burawoy in his endorsement of a 'public sociology':

> Between the organic public sociologist and a public is a dialogue, a process of mutual education. The recognition of public sociology must extend to the organic kind which often remains invisible, private, and is often considered to be apart from our professional lives. The project of such public sociologies is to make visible the invisible, to make the private public, to validate these organic connections as part of our sociological life. (Burawoy 2005: 8)

Insights I gained through personal experience created an opportunity to rethink the private/public boundary in the context of decision-making by public authorities. Mistakes and failures happen, and we must be alert and sympathetic to human fallibility, but my interest grew as I realised that what mattered was not so much the episode, as subsequent concealment. The involvement in this process of people who appeared genuinely unaware of their contribution to concealment further encouraged my sociological interest. This intensified as contrasts emerged between publicly available information and the concealed information disclosed through FOIA requests. Refusal of some requests on the grounds the information sought was 'personal' accelerated my thinking that this was a public issue of interest. Social research has a contribution to make to a democratic society, one element of which is enhancing knowledge about decision-making by those in positions of power. There will be tensions, as boundaries are contested and shift, but genuine protection of privacy can coexist alongside effective scrutiny and public accountability.

References

Bachrach, P., & Baratz, M. S. (1962). Two Faces of Power. *The American Political Science Review, 56*(4), 947–952.

Benhabib, S. (1992). *Situating the Self: Gender, Community and Postmodernism in Contemporary Ethics.* Cambridge: Polity Press.

Birchall, C. (2011). The Politics of Opacity and Openness. *Theory, Culture and Society, 28*(7), 7–25.

Blair, T. (2010). *A Journey.* London: Arrow Books.

Blair, T. (2012, July). *Letter from the Rt Hon Tony Blair to the Rt Hon Sir Alan Beith MP, Chair, Justice Committee.* Post-legislative Scrutiny of the Freedom of Information Act 200. https://publications.parliament.uk/pa/cm201213/cmselect/cmjust/96/tb01.htm

Blau, J., & Moncada, A. (2009). Sociological Theory and Human Rights: Two Logics, One World. In B. S. Turner (Ed.), *The New Blackwell Companion to Social Theory* (pp. 496–512). Chichester: Wiley-Blackwell.

Blom-Cooper, L. (1985). *A Child in Trust: The Report of the Panel of Inquiry into the Circumstances Surrounding the Death of Jasmine Beckford.* London: London Borough of Brent.

Blumer, H. (1969/1986). *Symbolic Interactionism: Perspective and Method.* Berkeley: University of California Press.

Brewer, J. (1984). Looking Back at Fascism: A Phenomenological Analysis of BUF Membership. *The Sociological Review, 32*(4), 742–760.

Brewer, J. (2004). Imagining The Sociological Imagination: The Biographical Context of a Sociological Classic. *The British Journal of Sociology, 55*(3), 317–333.

Brewer, J. (2005). The Public and Private in C. Wright Mills's Life and Work. *Sociology, 39*(4), 661–677.

Burawoy, M. (2005). For Public Sociology: 2004 Presidential Address. *American Sociological Review, 70*(1), 4–28.

Campaign for Freedom of Information. (2009, June 10). *Press Notice, Concern over New Freedom of Information Exemptions.* London.

Cladis, M. S. (1995). Durkheim's Communitarian Defence of Liberalism. In P. Hamilton (Ed.), *Emile Durkheim: Critical Assessments.* London: Routledge.

Duranti, M. (2012). Curbing Labour's Totalitarian Temptation: European Human Rights Law and British Postwar Politics. *Humanity: An International Journal of Human Rights, Humanitarianism, and Development, 3*(3), 361–383.

Elshtain, J. B. (1997). The Displacement of Politics. In Weintraub & Kumar (Eds.).

Farrand QC, J. (2016, July). Misguided Protection of Personal Data. *Public Law*, 383–392.

Frank, A. (2013). *The Wounded Storyteller: Body Illness and Ethics* (2nd ed.). Chicago/London: University of Chicago Press.

Fraser, N. (1998). Sex, Lies, and the Public Sphere: Reflections on the Confirmation of Clarence Thomas. In Landes (Ed.) (1998, pp. 314–337).

Freidson, E. (1970a). *Profession of Medicine: A Study of the Sociology of Applied Knowledge*. New York: Dodd, Mead.

Freidson, E. (1970b). *Professional Dominance*. Chicago: Atherton.

Freidson, E. (2001). *Professionalism: The Third Logic*. Cambridge: Polity Press.

Gallie, W. B. (1956). Essentially Contested Concepts. *Proceedings of the Aristotelian Society, 56*(1956), 167–198.

Gerth, H. H., & Mills, C. W. (Eds.). (1946). *From Max Weber: Essays in Sociology*. London: Routledge & Kegan Paul.

Goffman, E. (1959/1990). *The Presentation of Self in Everyday Life*. London: Penguin.

Hazell, R., & Worthy, B. (2009, September). *Impact of FOI on Central Government Constitution Unit End of Award Report to ESRC*. RES 062 23 0164.

Information Commissioner. (2009, June 10). *House of Commons Ministerial Veto on Disclosure of Cabinet Minutes Concerning Military Action Against Iraq Information Commissioner's Report to Parliament*. The Stationery Office HC622. Wilmslow, Cheshire, UK.

Information Commissioner. (2012) *Ministerial Veto on Disclosure of the Department of Health's Transition Risk Register: Information Commissioner's Report to Parliament*. The Stationery Office. Wilmslow, Cheshire, UK.

Landes, J. B. (Ed.). (1998). *Feminism, the Public and the Private*. Oxford: Oxford University Press.

Marx, K. (1843). *Critique of Hegel's Philosophy of Right*. Accessed online: https://www.marxists.org/archive/marx/works/download/Marx_Critique_of_Hegels_Philosophy_of_Right.pdf

Mills, C. W. (1959/2000). *The Sociological Imagination*. Oxford: Oxford University Press.

Ministry of Justice. (2009). Exercise of the Executive Override in Respect of the Decision of the Information Commissioner FS50165372 as Upheld by the Decision of the Information Tribunal EA/2008/0024 & EA/2008/0029. Statement of Reasons. Ministry of Justice.

Morgan, G. (1986). *Images of Organization*. Beverley Hills: Sage.

Mouffe, C. (2018). *For a Left Populism*. London: Verso.

Munroe, E. (2011). *The Munro Review of Child Protection: Final Report a Child-Centred System*. London: The Department for Education.

Rosenbaum, M. (2009, June 10). Government Plans FOI Restrictions BBC Open Secrets. http://www.bbc.co.uk/blogs/opensecrets/2009/06/government_plans_foi_restrictions.html

UCL Constitution Unit. (2016). *Disruptive or Beneficial? Freedom of Information in the UK*. https://constitution-unit.com/2016/03/09/disruptive-or-beneficial-freedom-of-information-in-the-uk/

Vaughan, D. (1996). *The Challenger Launch Decision*. Chicago: University of Chicago Press.

References

Abrams, P. (1988, March). Notes on the Difficulty of Studying the State (1977). *Journal of Historical Sociology, 1*(1), 58–89.

Adams, J. (2011). *Tony Benn: A Biography*. New York: Biteback Publishing.

Anderson, L. (2006). Analytic Autoethnography. *Journal of Contemporary Ethnography, 35*, 373–395.

Appointments Commission. (2011). *Review of the Appointment of xxxx as Chair of xxxx Trust*. Leeds: Appointments Commission.

Ashworth, J. (2002). *Human Rights, Serious Crime and Criminal Procedure. The Hamlyn Lectures*. London: Sweet & Maxwell.

Assinder, N. (1999, July 7). Blair Risks Row Over Public Sector. *BBC News*. http://news.bbc.co.uk/1/hi/uk_politics/388528.stm

Bachrach, P., & Baratz, M. S. (1962). Two Faces of Power. *The American Political Science Review, 56*(4), 947–952.

Bailey, J. (2000). Some Meanings of "The Private" in Sociological Thought. *Sociology, 34*(3), 381–401.

Ball, C. A. (2015). The Public Life of Secrets: Deception, Disclosure, and the Discursive Framing in the Policy Process. *Sociological Theory, 33*(2), 97–124.

Becker, H. (1967). Whose Side Are We On? *Social Problems, 14*(3), 234–247.

Benhabib, S. (1992). *Situating the Self: Gender, Community and Postmodernism in Contemporary Ethics*. Cambridge: Polity Press.

Benn, T. (1988). *Office Without Power: Diaries 1968–72*. London: Hutchinson.

Birchall, C. (2011). The Politics of Opacity and Openness. *Theory, Culture and Society, 28*(7), 7–25.

Blair, T. (2010). *A Journey*. London: Arrow Books.

M. Sheaff, *Secrecy, Privacy and Accountability*,
https://doi.org/10.1007/978-3-030-11686-6

Blair, T. (2012, July). *Letter from the Rt Hon Tony Blair to the Rt Hon Sir Alan Beith MP, Chair, Justice Committee*. Post-legislative Scrutiny of the Freedom of Information Act 200. https://publications.parliament.uk/pa/cm201213/cmselect/cmjust/96/tb01.htm

Blau, J., & Moncada, A. (2009). Sociological Theory and Human Rights: Two Logics, One World. In B. S. Turner (Ed.), *The New Blackwell Companion to Social Theory* (pp. 496–512). Chichester: Wiley-Blackwell.

Blom-Cooper, L. (1985). *A Child in Trust: The Report of the Panel of Inquiry into the Circumstances Surrounding the Death of Jasmine Beckford*. London: London Borough of Brent.

Blumer, H. (1969/1986). *Symbolic Interactionism: Perspective and Method*. Berkeley: University of California Press.

Bourdieu, P. (1989). Social Space and Symbolic Power. *Sociological Theory, 7*(1), 14–25.

Bovens, M. (1998). *The Quest for Responsibility: Accountability and Citizenship in Complex Organisations*. Cambridge: Cambridge University Press.

Breathnach, A. S., Riley, P. A., & Planche, T. D. (2011). Use of Freedom of Information Act to Produce Research on the Cheap? *British Medical Journal, 343*. https://doi.org/10.1136/bmj.d6129. Published 27 September 2011.

Brewer, J. (1984). Looking Back at Fascism: A Phenomenological Analysis of BUF Membership. *The Sociological Review, 32*(4), 742–760.

Brewer, J. (2004). Imagining The Sociological Imagination: The Biographical Context of a Sociological Classic. *The British Journal of Sociology, 55*(3), 317–333.

Brewer, J. (2005). The Public and Private in C. Wright Mills's Life and Work. *Sociology, 39*(4), 661–677.

British Sociological Association. (2017). *Statement of Ethical Practice for the British Sociological Association*. Durham, UK: British Sociological Association.

Brown, K. J. (2009, February). Freedom of Information as a Research Tool: Realising Its Potential. *The Howard Journal of Crime and Justice, 48*(1), 88–91.

Bulmer, M. (1982). The Merits and Demerits of Covert Participant Observation. In M. Bulmer (Ed.), *Social Research Ethics: An Examination of the Merits of Covert Participant Observation* (pp. 217–251). New York: Holmes and Meier.

Burawoy, M. (2005). For Public Sociology: 2004 Presidential Address. *American Sociological Review, 70*(1), 4–28.

Cabinet Office. (2018). *Freedom of Information Statistics in Central Government for 2017*. London: Cabinet Office.

Camdessus, M. (1997, November 13). *Lessons from Southeast Asia*. Singapore: International Monetary Fund Press Briefing.

Campaign for Freedom of Information. (2009, June 10). *Press Notice, Concern over New Freedom of Information Exemptions*. London.

Carr, E. H. (1964). *What Is History?* Harmondsworth: Penguin.

Chancellor of the Duchy of Lancaster. (1998). *Your Right to Know. White Paper.* London: The Stationery Office.

Christie, B. (2011, September 5). Tobacco Company Makes Freedom of Information Request for University's Research. *British Medical Journal, 343*, d5655.

Cicourel, A. (1964). *Method and Measurement in Sociology.* New York: Free Press.

Cladis, M. S. (1995). Durkheim's Communitarian Defence of Liberalism. In P. Hamilton (Ed.), *Emile Durkheim: Critical Assessments.* London: Routledge.

Costas, J., & Grey, C. (2016). *Secrecy at Work: The Hidden Architecture of Organizational Life.* Stanford: Stanford University Press..

Cowburn, A. (2018, April 23). Majority of People Think UK Government Should Fine Facebook After Data Scandal, Poll Reveals. *The Independent.*

Craib, I. (1997). *Classical Social Theory: An Introduction to the Thought of Marx, Weber, Durkheim and Simmel.* Oxford: Oxford University Press.

Curran, J. (Ed.). (1984). *The Future of the Left.* Oxford/Cambridge: Polity Press/ Basil Blackwell.

Davies, Sir H. E. (Chairman) (1967). *Report of the Tribunal Appointed to Inquire into the Disaster at Aberfan on October 21st, 1966.* London: Her Majesty's Stationery Office. http://www.mineaccidents.com.au/uploads/aberfan-report-original.pdf)

Davies, W. (2015). The Chronic Social: Relations of Control Within and Without Neoliberalism. *New Formations: A Journal of Culture/Theory Politics, 84*(85), 40–57.

Dawe, A. (1970). The Two Sociologies. *British Journal of Sociology, 21*, 207–218.

Deleuze, G. (1992, October). Postscript on Societies of Control. *October, 59*, 3–7.

den Heyer, G. (2010). New Public Management: A strategy for Democratic Police Reform in Transitioning and Developing Countries. *Policing: An International Journal of Police Strategies & Management, 34*(3), 419–433.

Department for Constitutional Affairs. (2006). *Freedom of Information Annual Report 2005: Operation of the FOI Act in Central Government.* London: Department for Constitutional Affairs.

Department of Health. (2000). *An Organisation with a Memory.* London: Department of Health.

Digman, J. M. (1990). Personality Structure: Emergence of the Five-Factor Model. *Annual Review of Psychology, 41*, 417–440.

Dobel, J. P. (1998). Judging the Private Lives of Public Officials. *Administration and Society, 30*(2), 115–142.

du Gay, P. (2008). Keyser Suze Elites: Market Populism and the Politics of International Change. *Sociological Review Monograph Series, 56*(1), 80–102.

Duranti, M. (2012). Curbing Labour's Totalitarian Temptation: European Human Rights Law and British Postwar Politics. *Humanity: An International Journal of Human Rights, Humanitarianism, and Development, 3*(3), 361–383.

Durkheim, E. (1893/1997). *The Division of Labour in Society*. New York: Free Press.

Dyer, C. (2001). Bristol Inquiry Condemns Hospital's "Club Culture". *British Medical Journal, 323*, 181.

Ellis, C. (1991). Sociological Introspection and Emotional Experience. *Symbolic Interaction, 14*(1), 23–50.

Elshtain, J. B. (1997). The Displacement of Politics. In Weintraub & Kumar (Eds.).

Etzioni, A. (2000). A Communitarian Perspective on Privacy. *Connecticut Law Review, 32*(3), 897–905.

Etzioni, A. (2010). Is Transparency the Best Disinfectant? *The Journal of Political Philosophy, 18*(4), 389–404.

Evans, M. (1993). Reading Lives: How the Personal Might Be Social. *Sociology, 27*(1), 5–13.

Exton, R. (2008). The Entrepreneur: A New Breed of Health Service Leader? *Journal of Health Organization and Management, 22*(3), 208–222.

Farrand QC, J. (2016, July). Misguided Protection of Personal Data. *Public Law*, 383–392.

Foucault, M. (1980). The Eye of Power. In C. Gordon (Ed.), *Power/Knowledge: Selected Interviews and Other Writings* (pp. 1972–1977). New York: Pantheon Books.

Fowler, A. J., Agha, R. A., Camm, C. F., & Littlejohns, P. (2013). The UK Freedom of Information Act (2000) in Healthcare Research: A Systematic Review. *BMJ Open, 2013*, e002967. https://doi.org/10.1136/bmjopen-2013-002967.

Francis, R. (2013). *Report of the Mid Staffordshire NHS Foundation Trust Public Inquiry*. London: The Stationery Office.

Frank, A. (2013). *The Wounded Storyteller: Body Illness and Ethics* (2nd ed.). Chicago/London: University of Chicago Press.

Fraser, N. (1998). Sex, Lies, and the Public Sphere: Reflections on the Confirmation of Clarence Thomas. In Landes (Ed.) (1998, pp. 314–337).

Freidson, E. (1970a). *Profession of Medicine: A Study of the Sociology of Applied Knowledge*. New York: Dodd, Mead.

Freidson, E. (1970b). *Professional Dominance*. Chicago: Atherton.

Freidson, E. (2001). *Professionalism: The Third Logic*. Cambridge: Polity Press.

Friedman, N. L. (1990). Autobiographical Sociology. *The American Sociologist, 21*(1), 60–66.

Fuchs, C. (2011). Towards an Alternative Concept of Privacy. *Journal of Information, Communication and Ethics in Society, 9*(4), 220–237.

Gallie, W. B. (1956). Essentially Contested Concepts. *Proceedings of the Aristotelian Society, 56*(1956), 167–198.

Gammell, C. (2008, December 8). Sharon Shoesmith Sacked After Baby P Scandal. *The Daily Telegraph*.

Garfinkel, H. (1967/1984). *Studies in Ethnomethodology*. Cambridge: Polity Press.
Gavison, R. (1980). Privacy and the Limits of Law. *The Yale Law Journal, 89*(3), 421–471.
Geneiys, W., & Hassenteufel, P. (2015). The Shaping of New State Elites: Healthcare Policymaking in France Since 1981. *Comparative Politics, 47*(3), 280–295.
Gerth, H. H., & Mills, C. W. (Eds.). (1946). *From Max Weber: Essays in Sociology*. London: Routledge & Kegan Paul.
Gibson, D. R. (2014). Enduring Illusions: The Social Organization of Secrecy and Deception. *Sociological Theory, 32*(4), 283–306.
Giddens, A. (2000). *The Third Way and Its Critics*. Cambridge: Polity Press.
Glancy, D. J. (1979). The Invention of the Right to Privacy. *Arizona Law Review, 21*(1), 1–37.
Goffman, E. (1959/1990). *The Presentation of Self in Everyday Life*. London: Penguin.
Gould, M. (2009, November 18). An Ill Wind Blows for Social Enterprise. *The Guardian*.
Gusterson, H. (1997). Studying Up Revisited. *Political and Legal Anthropology Review, 20*(1), 114–119.
Halford (2015, July 30). Big Data and the Politics of Discipline. *Discover Society*. Available at: http://discoversociety.org/2015/07/30/big-data-and-the-politics-of-discipline/
Halford, S., & Leonard, P. (2008). Place, Space and Time: Contextualizing Workplace Subjectivities. *Organization Studies, 27*(5), 657–676.
Hazell, R., & Worthy, B. (2009, September). *Impact of FOI on Central Government Constitution Unit End of Award Report to ESRC*. RES 062 23 0164.
Health Services Journal. (2007, February 15). After Eden, Things Look Rosy in the Social Enterprise Garden. *Health Service Journal*. https://www.hsj.co.uk/news/after-eden-things-look-rosy-in-the-social-enterprise-garden/1640.article
Held, D., & Keane, J. (1984). Socialism and the Limits of State Action. In Curran (Ed.).
Her Majesty's Inspector of Prisons (HMIP). (2004). *Report on an Announced Inspection of HMP Wandsworth 17–21 May 2004 by HM Chief Inspector of Prisons*. London: HMIP.
Her Majesty's Inspector of Prisons. (2006). *Report on a Full Follow-Up Inspection of HMP Wandsworth 10–14 July 2006 by HM Chief Inspector of Prisons*. London: HMIP.
Her Majesty's Inspectors of Prisons. (2009). *Report of an Announced Inspection of HMP Wandsworth (1–5 June 2009) by HM Chief Inspector of Prisons*. London: HMIP.

Hern, A., & Pegg, D. (2018, July 11). Facebook Fined for Data Breaches in Cambridge Analytica Scandal. *The Guardian*.

HM Government. (2010). *The Coalition: Our Programme for Government*. London: Cabinet Office.

Hochschild, A. R. (1983). *The Managed Heart: Commercialization of Human Feeling*. Berkeley: University of California Press.

Holmes, M. (2000). When Is the Personal Political? The President's Penis and Other Stories. *Sociology, 34*(2), 305–321.

House of Commons Committee on Standards and Privileges. (2010). *Ninth Report: Sir John Butterfill, Mr Stephen Byers, Ms Patricia Hewitt, Mr Geoff Hoon, Mr Richard Caborn and Mr Adam Ingram* (Vol. 2). London: House of Commons.

Hughes, K. (2015). The Social Value of Privacy, the Value of Privacy to Society and Human Rights Discourse. In Roessler & Mokrosinska (Eds.).

Information Commissioner. (2009, June 10). *House of Commons Ministerial Veto on Disclosure of Cabinet Minutes Concerning Military Action Against Iraq Information Commissioner's Report to Parliament*. The Stationery Office HC622. Wilmslow, Cheshire, UK.

Information Commissioner. (2012) *Ministerial Veto on Disclosure of the Department of Health's Transition Risk Register: Information Commissioner's Report to Parliament*. The Stationery Office. Wilmslow, Cheshire, UK.

Information Commissioner. (2018a, June 11). *Investigation into the Use of Data Analytics in Political Campaigns Investigation Update*. Wilmslow, Cheshire, UK.

Information Commissioner (2018b, July 11). *Democracy Disrupted? Personal Information and Political Influence*. Wilmslow, Cheshire, UK.

Information Commissioner of Canada. (1998). *Annual Report*.

Jamieson, L. (2011). Intimacy as a Concept: Explaining Social Change in the Context of Globalisation or Another Form of Ethnocentricism? *Sociological Research Online, 16*(4).

Johnson, D., & Hampson, E. (2015). Utilising the UK Freedom of Information Act 2000 for Crime Record Data: Indications of the Strength of Records Management in Day to Day Police Business. *Records Management Journal, 25*(3), 248–268.

Jones, L., & Exworthy, M. (2015). Framing in Policy Processes: A Case Study from Hospital Planning in the National Health Service in England. *Social Science and Medicine, 124*(2015), 196–204.

Jupp, V., & Norris, C. (1993). Traditions in Documentary Analysis. In M. Hammersely (Ed.), *Social Research: Philosophy, Politics and Practice*. London: SAGE Publications.

Kasper, D. V. S. (2005, March). The Evolution (or Devolution) of Privacy. *Sociological Forum, 20*(1), 69–92.

Keen, M. F. (1992). The Freedom of Information Act and Sociological Research. *The American Sociologist, 23*(2), 43–51.

Keen, M. F. (2004). *Stalking Sociologists: J Edgar Hoover's FBI Surveillance of American Sociology*. New Brunswick: Transaction Publishers.

Kelner, S. (2018, December 26). The Case of Paul Gait and Elaine Kirt Shows That the Rush to Judgement Can Make Morons of Us All. *iNews*.

Landes, J. B. (Ed.). (1998). *Feminism, the Public and the Private*. Oxford: Oxford University Press.

Latour, B. (2007, April 6). Beware your imagination leaves digital traces. *Times Higher Education Supplement*.

Lee, R. M. (2005). The UK Freedom of Information Act and Social Research. *International Journal of Social Research Methodology: Theory and Practice, 8*(1), 1–18.

Lemke. (2001). 'The Birth of Bio-Politics': Michel Foucault's Lecture at the Collège de France on Neo liberal Governmentality. *Economy and Society, 30*(2), 190–207.

Letherby, G. (2013). Theorised Subjectivity. In G. Letherby, J. Scott, & M. Williams (Eds.), *Objectivity and Subjectivity in Social Research*. London: Sage.

Levenson, The Rt Hon Lord Justice. (2012). *An Inquiry into the Culture, Practices and Ethics of the Press*. London: The Stationery Office.

Lever, A. (2015). Privacy, democracy and Freedom of Expression. In Roessler & Mokrosinska (Eds.).

Lewis, W. (2019, May 2). MP's Expenses: A Very British Scandal. *New Statesman*.

Leys, C. (1984). The Rise of the Authoritarian State. In J. Curran (Ed.).

Luscombe, A. (2018). Deception Declassified: The Social Organisation of Cover Storying in a Secret Intelligence Operation. *Sociology, 52*(2), 400–415.

Luscombe, A., Walby, K., & Lippert, R. K. (2017). Brokering Access Beyond the Border and in the Wild: Comparing Freedom of Information Law and Policy in Canada and the United States. *Law & Policy, 39*(3), 259–279.

Maclean, I., & Johnes, M. (2000). *Aberfan: Government and Disasters*. Cardiff: Welsh Academic Press.

Macpherson, C. B. (1962). *The Political Theory of Possessive Individualism: From Hobbes to Locke*. Oxford: Oxford University Press.

Manovich, L. (2011). The *Promises and the Challenges of Big Social Data*. http://manovich.net/content/04-projects/067-trending-the-promises-and-the-challenges-of-big-social-data/64-article-2011.pdf

Marx, K. (1843). *Critique of Hegel's Philosophy of Right*. Accessed online: https://www.marxists.org/archive/marx/works/download/Marx_Critique_of_Hegels_Philosophy_of_Right.pdf

McGuigan, J. (2014). The Neoliberal Self. *Culture Unbound, 6*, 223–240.

McNay, L. (2009). Self as Enterprise: Dilemmas of Control and Resistance in Foucault's the Birth of Biopolitics. *Theory, Culture and Society, 26*(6), 55–77.

Meijer, A. (2014). Transparency. In M. Bovens, R. E. Goodin, & T. Schillemans (Eds.), *The Oxford Handbook of Public Accountability* (pp. 507–524). Oxford: Oxford University Press.

Miliband, R. (1970). The Capitalist State: Reply to Nicos Poulantzas. *New Left Review, 59*, 53–70.

Miliband, R. (1973). *The State in Capitalist Society: The Analysis of the Western System of Power*. London: Quartet Books.

Mill, J. S., & Lerner, M. (1965). *Essential Works of John Stuart Mill*. New York: Bantam Books.

Mills, C. W. (1956/2000). *The Power Elite* (New ed.). Oxford: Oxford University Press.

Ministry of Justice. (2009). Exercise of the Executive Override in Respect of the Decision of the Information Commissioner FS50165372 as Upheld by the Decision of the Information Tribunal EA/2008/0024 & EA/2008/0029. Statement of Reasons. Ministry of Justice.

Mokrosinska, D. (2015). How Much Privacy for Public Officials? In Roessler & Mokrosinska (Eds.).

Moore, S. (2018). Towards a Sociology of Institutional Transparency: Openness, Deception and the Problem of Public Trust. *Sociology, 52*(2), 416–430.

Morgan, G. (1986). *Images of Organization*. Beverley Hills: Sage.

Mouffe, C. (2018). *For a Left Populism*. London: Verso.

Munroe, E. (2011). *The Munro Review of Child Protection: Final Report a Child-Centred System*. London: The Department for Education.

Murray, C. (2013). Sport in Care: Using Freedom of Information Requests to Elicit Data about Looked After Children's Involvement in Physical Activity. *British Journal of Social Work, 43*, 1347–1363.

Nader, L. (1969/1972). Up the Anthropologist: Perspectives Gained from Studying Up. In D. Hymes (Ed.), *Reinventing Anthropology*. New York: Random House.

Nader, L. (1997). Controlling Processes: Tracing the Dynamic Processes of Power. *Current Anthropology, 38*(5), 711–738.

Nagel, T. (1998). Concealment and Exposure. *Philosophy and Public Affairs, 27*(1), 3–30.

National Audit Office. (2014). *Memorandum for the House of Commons Health Committee: Investigation into NHS Property Services Ltd*. London: National Audit Office.

NHS London Audit Consortium. (2010). *Secure Healthcare*. London: NHS London Audit Consortium.

NHS Wandsworth. (2009). *Prison Healthcare Services – Insolvency of Secure Healthcare Limited PCT Review*. London: NHS Wandsworth.

Offe, C. (1998). *The Present Historical Transformation and Some Basic Design Options for Social Institutions*. Cited in Giddens (2000: 56).
Oliver-Smith, A. (2011). Revealing Root Causes: The Disaster Anthropology of Gregory Button. *American Anthropologist, 113*(4), 646–648.
Pateman, C. (1989). *The Disorder of Women: Democracy, Feminism and Political Theory*. Cambridge: Polity Press.
Perrow, C. (1999). *Normal Accidents: Living with High Risk Technologies*. Princeton: Princeton University Press.
Peters, M. (2001). Education, Enterprise Culture and the Entrepreneurial Self: A Foucauldian Perspective. *Journal of Educational Enquiry, 2*(2), 58–71.
Platt, J. (1981). Evidence and Proof in Documentary Research: 1 Some Specific Problems of Documentary Research. *The Sociological Review, 29*(1), 31–52.
Plummer, K. (1983). *Documents of Life*. London: Allen and Unwin.
Plummer, K. (2001). *Documents of Life 2*. London: SAGE Publications.
Poulantzas, N. (1970). The Problem of the Capitalist State. *New Left Review, 58*, 67–78.
Power, M. (1999). *The Audit Society: Rituals of Verification*. Oxford: Oxford University Press.
Prior, L. (2003). *Using Documents in Social Research*. London: SAGE Publications.
Pyysiainen, J., Halpin, D., & Guilfoyle, A. (2017). Neoliberal Governance and 'Responsibilization' of Agents: Reassessing the Mechanisms of Responsibility-Shift in Neoliberal Discursive Environments. *Distinktion: Journal of Social Theory, 18*(2), 215–235.
Ramesh, R. (2011, August 2). Supreme Court Rejects Bid to Challenge Ruling on Sharon Shoesmith Sacking. *The Guardian*.
Reeves, A., Friedman, S., Rahal, C., & Reeves, M. F. (2017). The Decline and Persistence of the Old Boy: Private Schools and Elite Recruitment 1897 to 2016. *American Sociological Review, 82*(6), 1139–1166.
Ribbens-McCarthy, J., & Edwards, R. (2001). Illuminating Meanings of "The Private" in Sociological Thought. *Sociology, 35*(3), 765–777.
Roessler, B. (2015). Should Personal Data Be a Tradeable Good? On the Moral Limits of Markets in Privacy. In B. Roessler & D. Mokrosinska (Eds.), *Social Dimensions of Privacy: Interdisciplinary Perspectives*. Cambridge: Cambridge University Press.
Rogers de Waal. (2017). Security Trumps Privacy in British Attitudes to Cyber-Surveillance. *YouGov*. https://yougov.co.uk/news/2017/06/12/Security-Trumps-Privacy/
Rose, N. (1992). Governing the Enterprising Self. In P. Heelas & P. Morris (Eds.), *The Values of the Enterprise Culture: The Moral Debate* (pp. 141–164). London: Routledge.
Rosenbaum, M. (2009, June 10). Government Plans FOI Restrictions BBC Open Secrets. http://www.bbc.co.uk/blogs/opensecrets/2009/06/government_plans_foi_restrictions.html

Rossler, B. (2005). *The Value of Privacy* (R. D. V. Glasgow, Trans.). Cambridge: Polity Press.

Royal College of Nursing. (2007, February). *Policy Briefing: Social Enterprise Update.* London: RCN.

Savage, A., & Hyde, R. (2014). Using Freedom of Information Requests to Facilitate Research. *International Journal of Social Research Methodology, 17*(3), 303–317. https://doi.org/10.1080/13645579.2012.742280.

Savage, M., & Williams, K. (2008). Elites: Remembered in Capitalism and Forgotten by Social Sciences. *Sociological Review Monograph Series, 56*(1), 1–24.

Savage, M., Devin, F., Cunningham, N., Taylor, M., Li, Y., Hjellbrekke, J., Le Roux, B., Friedman, S., & Miles, A. (2013). A New Model of Social Class?: Findings from the BBC's Great British Class Survey Experiment. *Sociology, 47*, 1–32.

Schattschneider, E. E. (1960). *The Semi-Sovereign People.* New York: Holy, Rinehart and Winston.

Scott, J. (1990). *A Matter of Record: Documentary Sources in Social Research.* Cambridge: Polity Press.

Scott, J. (2008). Modes of Power and the Re-Conceptualization of Elites. *Sociological Review Monograph Series, 56*(1), 27–43.

Scraton, P. (2004). Speaking Truth to Power: Experiencing Critical Research. In M. Smyth & E. Wiliamson (Eds.), *Researchers and Their 'Subjects': Ethics, Power, Knowledge and Consent.* Bristol: The Policy Press.

Secretary of State for Health. (2006). *Our Health, Our Care, Our Say: A New Direction for Community Services.* London: HMSO.

Secure Healthcare Ltd. (2009a). *Annual Return and Accounts.* London: Secure Healthcare.

Secure Healthcare Ltd. (2009b, September 9). *Report to SHL Board of Directors.* London: Meeting.

Shaw, E. (2004). What Matters Is What Works: The Third Way and the Case of the Private Finance Initiative. In S. Hale, W. Leggett, & L. Martell (Eds.), *The Third Way and Beyond: Criticisms, Futures, Alternatives* (pp. 64–82). Manchester: Manchester University Press.

Sheaff, M. (1988). NHS Ancillary Services and Competitive Tendering. *Industrial Relations Journal, 19*(2), 93–105.

Sheaff, M. (2017). Constructing Accounts of Organisational Failure: Policy, Power and Concealment. *Critical Social Policy, 37*(4), 520–539.

Shils, E. A. (1956). Two Patterns of Publicity, Secrecy and Privacy. *Bulletin of the Atomic Scientists, 12*(6), 215–220.

Shils, E. (1966). Privacy: Its Constitution and Vicissitudes. *Law and Contemporary Problems, 31*, 281–306.

Shore, C., & Wright, S. (1997). *Anthropology of Policy: Perspectives on Governance and Power.* London: Routledge.

Simmel, G. (1906). The Sociology of Secrecy and of Secret Societies. *The American Journal of Sociology, 11*(4), 441–498.
Simonet, D. (2011). The New Public Management Theory and the Reform of European Health Care Systems: An International Comparative Perspective. *International Journal of Public Administration, 34*(12), 815–826.
South West London & St George's NHS Mental Health Trust (SWL&SG). (2011). *Secure Healthcare: Report to Audit Committee.* SWL&SG.
Standing, G. (2011). *The Precariat: The New Dangerous Class.* London: Bloomsbury Academic.
Stanley, L. (1993). On Auto/Biography in Sociology. *Sociology, 27*(1), 41–52.
Taylor, A. (2007, July 2). Prison Health Contract Goes to Secure Healthcare. *Community Care.*
Thompson, D. F. (1980, December). Moral Responsibility of Public Officials: The Problem of Many Hands. *The American Political Science Review, 74*(4), 905–916A.
Thompson, J. B. (2005). The New Visibility. *Theory, Culture and Society, 22*(6), 31–51.
Thompson, J. B. (2011). Shifting Boundaries of Public and Private Life. *Theory, Culture and Society, 28*(4), 49–70.
Thompson, D. F. (2014, May). Responsibility for Failures of Government: The Problem of Many Hands. *American Journal of Public Administration, 44*(3), 259–227.
Tombs, S. (2018). The UK's Corporate Killing Law: Un/Fit for Purpose? *Criminology & Criminal Justice, 18*(4), 488–507.
Tribal Newchurch. (2009). *Social Enterprise Pathfinder Programme Evaluation Report 4 – Final Report.* London.
Turner, B. (1976, September). The Organizational and Interorganizational Development of Disasters. *Administrative Science Quarterly, 1*, 378–397.
Turner, B. S. (1993). Outline of a Theory of Human Rights. *Sociology, 27*(3), 489–512.
Turner, C. (2017, December 22). The High Profile People That Supported Charles Howeson During His Trial. *Plymouth Herald.* https://www.plymouthherald.co.uk/news/plymouth-news/high-profile-people-supported-charles-968857
UCL Constitution Unit. (2016). *Disruptive or Beneficial? Freedom of Information in the UK.* https://constitution-unit.com/2016/03/09/disruptive-or-beneficial-freedom-of-information-in-the-uk/
Vallas, S. P., & Cummins, E. R. (2015). Personal Branding and Identity Norms in the Popular Business Press: Enterprise Culture in an Age of Precarity. *Organization Studies, 36*(3), 293–319.
Vaughan, D. (1996). *The Challenger Launch Decision.* Chicago: University of Chicago Press.

Vaughan, D. (1999). The Dark Side of Organizations: Mistake, Misconduct and Disaster. *Annual Review of Sociology, 25*, 271–305.

Wacquant, L. (1992). Methodological Relationism. In P. Bourdieu & L. Wacquant (Eds.), *An Invitation to Reflexive Sociology*. Cambridge/Oxford: Polity Press/Blackwell.

Walby, K., & Larsen, M. (2011). Getting at the Live Archive: On Access to Information Research in Canada. *Canadian Journal of Law and Society, 26*(3), 623–634.

Walby, K., & Larsen, M. (2012). Access to Information and Freedom of Information Requests: Neglected Means of Data Production in the Social Sciences. *Qualitative Inquiry, 18*(1), 31–42.

Walby, K., & Luscombe, A. (2017). Criteria for Quality in Qualitative Research and Use of Freedom of Information Requests in Social Research. *Qualitative Research, 17*(5), 537–553.

Wandsworth PCT (2009). *Minutes of Wandsworth PCT Community Services Board*, 17 November 2009. London: Wandsworth PCT.

Wandsworth PCT (2010). *Minutes of Wandsworth PCT Community Services Board*, 19 January 2010. London: Wandsworth PCT.

Warner, J. (2015). *The Emotional Politics of Social Work and Child Protection*. Bristol: Policy Press.

Warren, S. D., & Brandeis, L. D. (1890). The Right to Privacy. *Harvard Law Review, 4*(5), 193–220.

Watson, T. J. (2008). Managing Identity: Identity Work, Personal Predicaments and Structural Circumstances. *Organization, 15*(1), 121–143.

Weintraub, J. (1997). The Theory and Politics of the Public/Private Distinction. In Weintraub and Kumar (Eds.).

Weintraub, J., & Kumar, K. (Eds.). (1997). *Public and Private in Thought and Practice*. Chicago/London: University of Chicago Press.

Westin, A. F. (1967). *Privacy and Freedom*. London: The Bodley Head.

Wilensky, H. L. (1967). *Organizational Intelligence*. New York: Basic Books.

Wilks-Heeg, S. (2015). Revolving Door Politics and Corruption. In D. Whyte (Ed.), *How Corrupt Is Britain?* London: Pluto Press.

Williams, R. (1983). *Keywords: A Vocabulary of Culture and Society*. London: Flamingo Press.

YouGov. (2018, July 23). Most Brits Think Police Suspects Are Entitled to Privacy Until They Are Found Guilty of a Crime. *YouGov*. https://yougov.co.uk/news/2018/07/23/most-brits-think-suspects-entitled-privacy/

Young, H. (1999, May 25). The Final Triumph of All the Butchers and Whisperers. *The Guardian*.

Younger, K. (Chairman) (1973). *Report of the Committee on Privacy*. Presented to Parliament, July 1972. London: HMSO.

Zerubavel, E. (1997). *Social Mindscapes: An Invitation to Cognitive Sociology*. Cambridge, MA/London: Harvard University Press.

Index

M. Sheaff, *Secrecy, Privacy and Accountability*,
https://doi.org/10.1007/978-3-030-11686-6